HURRICANE KATRINA

Response and Responsibilities

John Brown Childs
editor

new pacific press
Santa Cruz, California
2005

Published and distributed in the United States by
New Pacific Press
204 Locust Street
Santa Cruz, CA 95060

www.literaryguillotine.com/npp/npphome.html

First published 2005

10 9 8 7 6 5 4 3 2 1

New Pacific Press was established in 2003 as a "Hey, we'll at
least break even" alternative to the commercial, homogeneous
publications that currently dominate the publishing industry.
New Pacific Press does not believe that it necessarily serves the
public interest to operate a not-for-profit enterprise, but rather
that there is both value and viability in publishing small, innovative,
educational and culturally significant works that the mainstream
may consider small potatoes. Our planned publications will be
primarily sociopolitical, economic, cultural studies; they will
be scholarly, personal, poetic, mixed-media presentations that
reflect the multiplicity of cultural work being done in the greater
Bay Area and throughout the Pacific Rim(s).

"Saving America's Soul Kitchen" by Wynton Marsalis © 2005
Time Inc., reprinted by permission

The essay "Empower the Poor or the Fire Next Time" is reprinted
by permission of Grace Lee Boggs and the *Michigan Citizen*

The essay "Thinking for Ourselves: Fundamental Questions" is
reprinted by permission of Shea Howell and the *Michigan Citizen*

Book design by Stephen Pollard
Set in Warnock Pro and Silentium Pro

Cover photo by James Nielsen © Getty Images

ISBN 0-9712546-2-1

Printed in Canada by Hemlock Printers Ltd.

I think at this stage the big question is,
What is the American society?
Is it the kind of society . . . that permits people
to grow and develop according to their capacity,
that gives them a sense of value, not only for themselves,
but a sense of value for other human beings?
Is this the kind of society that is going to permit that?
I think there is a great question
as to whether it can become that kind of society.

—Ella Jo Baker,
African American, civil rights organizer, cofounder of the
Student Nonviolent Coordinating Committee (SNCC),
speaking at the Institute for the Black World,
Atlanta, Georgia, 1969.*

---

*This speech can be found in Joanne Grant's *Ella Baker: Freedom Bound,* John Wiley and Sons, New York (1998).

Acknowledgements

This book is made possible by David S. Watson, proprietor of The Literary Guillotine bookstore, and the creative founder of the innovative not-for-profit New Pacific Press in Santa Cruz. Thanks to Stephen Pollard for the excellent design and production work. Thanks also to John Flynn-York for his careful proofreading. Delgra Childs provided valuable suggestions. Wynton Marsalis graciously agreed to the inclusion of his essay, originally published in *Time* magazine. *Time* granted permission to reprint that essay. I also thank the efficient and helpful Isobel Allen-Floyd at Wynton Marsalis Enterprises, and Kelley Gately at *Time,* for their assistance. The *Michigan Citizen* gave permission to reprint the works by Grace Lee Boggs and Sharon Howell. Thanks to Teresa Maxwell-Kelly, Editor of that newspaper, and to Grace and Sharon. Rev. Nelson Johnson and the Interfaith Workers Justice network generously allowed the reprinting of their statement calling for "an ethical reconstruction commission" in New Orleans.

The Transcommunal Studies Cluster of the Chicano/Latino Research Center; the Center for Justice, Tolerance, and Community; and the Institute for Advanced Feminist Research, all at the University of California Santa Cruz, provided enabling financial support for this book.

And my deep appreciation to all those who contributed the essays that make up this book. Proceeds from sales of the book will be donated to the People's Hurricane Relief Fund, Vanguard Public Foundation.

Foreword

My intention in developing this book is to make available a wide range of accessible perspectives about the impact and significance of Hurricane Katrina. That disaster exposed and raised many difficult and core dilemmas facing New Orleans, the Gulf region, and the United States. So it is fitting that there be a variety of responses in this book that address the multifaceted question of responsibilities—not just about the causes, but also concerning that which we in the United States can do, indeed must do, to address underlying vulnerabilities stemming from deep-seated inequality in this country. With this intention, I invited a range of participants to contribute short essays that provide analysis and illumination about Katrina and its implications. These essays will help fill the space between the immediate journalism that emerged during the Katrina catastrophe and the more detailed writing that will undoubtedly appear in the next year or two. Because this book's writers make reference to discussions from a diverse range of sources, this book also provides a useful roadmap to some important analyses that came out soon after Katrina.

The essays speak for themselves. I invite you to hear their voices.

John Brown Childs
Santa Cruz, California
October 24, 2005,
United Nations Day

1

The New Battle for New Orleans

Paul Ortiz

The people of New Orleans will not go quietly into the night, scattering across this country to become homeless in countless other cities while federal relief funds are funneled into rebuilding casinos, hotels, chemical plants. We will not stand idly by while this disaster is used as an opportunity to replace our homes with newly built mansions and condos in a gentrified New Orleans.[1]
—Community Labor United, New Orleans

What happened to New Orleans is a bipartisan political crime. The people of the Gulf Coast paid the price for Bill Clinton's "the era of big government is over," and for the Republican dream of dragging government into the bathroom and drowning it to fund tax cuts for the wealthy, as enunciated by Grover Norquist. Recent Tulane Law School graduate Sacha Boegem described the scene:

---

[1]Cited in: Naomi Klein, "Let The People Rebuild New Orleans," www.thenation.com, September 8, 2005.

Tens of thousands of mostly poor, Black citizens trapped on rooftops, in attics, in hospitals, in the convention center, and in the Superdome. Trapped, day after awful day without food, water, medicine, working toilets, security, or help of any kind. Not in America we thought. Not in the land of the free, the richest nation on earth, the global superpower. Not here at home. But we were wrong.[2]

The presidential election of 2000 and the aftermath of Hurricane Katrina demonstrate that white supremacy and Jim Crow inequalities are alive and well in the United States. The disenfranchisement of thousands of African Americans in Florida set the stage for five more years of corporate rule, war profiteering, and policies that starved cities like New Orleans to death. Only a Black-majority city would be forced to suffer the indignity of being patrolled by private security forces just returned from their misadventures in Iraq.

The hurricane has blown away the illusion that racism is on the demise or that We Are All In This Together.[3] Actually, some of us are doing quite well while others are still catching hell. Some of us travel to foreign countries on inherited dimes while others can't afford cars. Some of us live on high ground in the suburbs while others are shunted into "the bottoms" or low ground. It is obscene to hear media experts claim that Hurricane Katrina has forced us to once again pay attention to race and class in America. That's all we have been doing for the past three decades. Between 1970 and 2000, public policies in the United States, ranging from urban development to education, were formulated more on the basis of enhancing the race and class privileges of the few rather than delivering the greatest good to the many. The major source of the social crisis we face today is that the major American political parties will do anything *but* rely on the wisdom of African Americans or working class people to

[2]Sacha Boegem, "Hurricane Bush," www.commondreams.org, September 13, 2005.

[3]Ishmael Reed, "Race, Katrina and the Media," www.counterpunch.org, September 16, 2005.

frame their policies. In this distorted practice it is the norm for the disenfranchised to be the *objects* of public policy, to be punished or uplifted by social policy, but *never* to have the right to be policy framers.

The backers and beneficiaries of George W. Bush are using the hurricane as an excuse to turn New Orleans into a laboratory for right-wing free market economics. Corporations as well as intellectual and financial elites are circling New Orleans like vultures. Real estate developers smell blood in the water. There's profits to be made from removing African Americans from the city and speculating on vacant properties. The hurricane has left the entire Gulf Coast vulnerable to ideologies we generally associate with the worst aspects of globalization such as privatization, tax-free enterprise zones, anti-labor policies, and the suspension of environmental regulations. These ideas have crippled economies around the world from Russia to Argentina, but they benefit the rich, and they will now be imposed on New Orleans. Even as the flood waters ebb, these feed-the-wealthy-more strategies are, according to Naomi Klein, "poised to become law or have already been adopted by presidential decree."[4] As Klein and others have reported, the larger goal seems to be the replacement of African-American neighborhoods with playgrounds for wealthy tourists. The chickens of globalization are returning to roost in the United States with a vengeance. New Orleans is ever more firmly joined with Chiapas, South Africa, Havana, South Korea and other locations as sites of struggle over the future of humanity. Perhaps the next World Social Forum should be held in New Orleans.

C. L. R. James argued that the more active the people are the more active government can be. Millions of people in this society believe in the kind of limited government that doomed New Orleans because their relationship to power in this society is one of complete submission. They are

---

[4]Naomi Klein, "Purging the Poor," www.thenation.com, October 10, 2005.

suspicious of government because they have no way of calling it into question other than participating in the occasional election or meaningless opinion poll. The goal of progressives now should be to create a nation where government is not the enemy or the problem, but rather a society where *government is the people and the people are the government.* The way to do this is to create and reinvigorate institutions such as unions, community organizations, and mutual aid associations that give ordinary people a sense of movement and a feeling of control over our everyday lives. In turn, these institutions provide us with enhanced power to challenge the ability of corporations and other elites to influence national politics.

Progressive social change occurs when poor and oppressed peoples in concert with other groups start new social movements. Mass movements have driven every great era of reform in this nation's history. The unemployment movements of the 1930s helped usher in the New Deal. African-American workers—domestics, janitors, and common laborers—were the heroes of the bus boycott campaigns which drove the civil rights movement. In 1965, Filipino and Mexican-American field hands started the farm worker movement, a mass struggle that lifted thousands of poor people out of poverty *simultaneously*.

Rev. Martin Luther King Jr. drew from these examples in order to create what he called "The Poor People's Campaign," a crusade to end poverty nationally. King's assassination obliterated not only the campaign but the truism that too many of us have forgotten: the most profound gains in dignity, justice and equality in US history have occurred when African Americans and other workers were gaining power. The loss of that power leads to despair, injustice, and a lack of *accountability* between all levels of society. Witness the lack of accountability in the initial Federal response to Katrina. No wonder that millions of people in this society believe that government is the problem.

What is at stake in the new Battle for New Orleans, and why should the readers of this essay care about the city's future? New Orleans has been the site of some of the deepest struggles against tyranny in the Western Hemisphere. During the period of slavery in the United States, slave masters forced slaves to live in the unhealthiest areas of plantations, near the malaria-ridden swamps or river bottom areas prone to disease and flooding. Masters in Louisiana and the deep South typically summered in Philadelphia or Paris while their workers dropped dead in the sugar or rice plantations.

In response to these conditions, enslaved Africans and Native Americans organized numerous revolts. Runaway slaves formed independent communities in the swamps surrounding New Orleans. Centuries before the rise of the global justice movement, some of these communities were in touch with revolutionaries in Haiti, Cuba, and other flashpoints of opposition to slavery and colonialism. During the Civil War, thousands of African Americans in the greater New Orleans area took up arms to save the union and to liberate their brothers and sisters. In the 1890s, local Black organizations launched campaigns against segregation, one of which went straight to the US Supreme Court and became known as *Plessy v. Ferguson.*

These stories were repressed or distorted by the United States during the Jim Crow period because they provided excellent models for oppressed peoples to challenge exploitation. The continuing denial of the importance of African-American history is equally pragmatic. Ignoring the narrative of African-American struggles today allows the dominant society to treat Black people as if they have no independent political history, no tradition of community organizing, no option other than to take whatever the government or private charities have in store for them. In contrast, the study of African-American history provides all of us—the people of New Orleans and the nation—with ways to re-imagine and reconstruct popular democracy in this country. Achieving this is no longer a matter of idealism; in the wake of Hurricane Katrina it is a matter of survival.

If we are to save New Orleans from becoming a gentrified haven for the elite we must insist that these hidden, glorious histories become part of the visible and educational landscape of the city and the nation. Here is one idea. Instead of merely building chain motels, casinos, and taverns for wealthy tourists why not create a National Museum of Segregation that tells the story of Homer Plessy, post-Reconstruction efforts of Black southerners to regain the vote, and the national crusade to end lynching? Instead of placing youths in dead-end service jobs, imagine putting them to work as history interns with digital tape recorders, cameras and other recording equipment in order to gather the oral histories of their elders who survived segregation. The museum would become part of a community-based campaign to gather and promote the proud history and culture of New Orleans and the Gulf Coast. School children would be taught documentary writing, film production, and technical skills that would make them excited about learning.

The struggle to save New Orleans from social, economic, and historical death is a defining moment for progressive activists. The reactionaries are coming to New Orleans in order to purge it of its 67% majority Black population, and they equally desire to purge it of its history. If we allow them to do a corporate makeover of New Orleans and transform it into a haven for the rich then they will use this triumph to impose a new wave of reactionary politics on the rest of the country. We must work in solidarity with our brothers and sisters in New Orleans and the Gulf Coast. In this time of crisis, we must support local, grassroots organizations in the region. Whatever they need, whatever they ask of us, we need to supply it.

2

Saving America's Soul Kitchen

How to bring this country together?
Listen to the message of New Orleans

Wynton Marsalis

Now the levee breach has been fixed. The people have been evacuated. Army Corps of Engineers magicians will pump the city dry, and the slow (but quicker than we think) job of rebuilding will begin. Then there will be no twenty-four-hour news coverage. The spin doctors' narrative will create a wall of illusion thicker than the new levees. The job of turning our national disaster into sound-bite-size commercials with somber string music will be left to TV. The story will be sanitized as our nation's politicians congratulate themselves on a job well done. Americans of all stripes will demonstrate saintly concern for one another. It's what we do in a crisis.

This tragedy, however, should make us take an account of ourselves. We should not allow the mythic significance of the moment to pass without proper consideration. Let us assess the size of this cataclysm in cultural terms, not in dollars and cents or politics. Americans are far less successful at doing that, because we have never understood how our core beliefs are manifest in culture, and how culture should guide political and economic realities. That's what the city of New Orleans can now teach the nation again as we are all forced by circumstances to literally come closer to one another. I say teach us again, because New Orleans is a true American melting pot: the soul of America. A place freer than the rest of the country, where elegance met an indefinable wildness to encourage the flowering of creative intelligence. Whites, Creoles and Negroes were strained, steamed, and stewed in a thick, sticky, below-sea-level bowl of musky gumbo. These people produced an original cuisine, an original architecture, vibrant communal ceremonies and an original art form: jazz.

Their music exploded irrepressibly from the forced integration of these castes to sweep the world as the definitive American art form. New Orleans, the Crescent City, the Big Easy—home of Mardi Gras, the second-line parade, the po'boy sandwich, the shotgun house—is so many people's favorite city. But not favorite enough to embrace the integrated superiority of its culture as a national objective. Not favorite enough to digest the gift of supersized soul internationally embodied by the great Louis Armstrong. Over time, New Orleans became known as the national center for frat-party-type decadence and (yeah, boy) great food. The genuine greatness of Armstrong is reduced to his good nature; his artistic triumphs are unknown to all but a handful. So it's time to consider, as we rebuild this great American city, exactly what this bayou metropolis symbolizes for the United States.

New Orleans has a habit of tweaking the national consciousness at pivotal times. The last foreign invasion on US soil was repelled in the Crescent City in 1815. The Union had an important early victory over the South with the capture of the Big Easy in 1862. Homer Plessy, a Black New Orleanian, fought for racial equality in 1896, although it took our Supreme Court fifty-eight years to agree with him and, with *Brown v. Board of Education,* to declare segregation unequal. Martin Luther King's Southern Christian Leadership Conference was formally organized in New Orleans in 1957. The problem is that we, all us Americans, have a tendency to rise in the moment of need, but when the moment passes, we fall back again.

The images of a ruined city make it clear that we need to rebuild New Orleans. The images of people stranded, in shock, indicate that we need to rebuild a community. The images of all sorts of Americans aiding these victims speak of the size of our hearts. But this time we need to look a little deeper. Let's use the resurrection of the city to reacquaint the country with the gift of New Orleans: a multicultural community invigorated by the arts. Forget about tolerance. What about embracing? This tragedy implores us to re-examine the soul of America. Our democracy has from its very beginnings been challenged by the shackles of slavery. The parade of Black folks across our TV screens asking, as if ghosts, "Have you seen my father, mother, sister, brother?" reconnects us all to the still unfulfilled goals of the Reconstruction era. We always back away from fixing our nation's racial problems. Not fixing the city's levees before Katrina struck will now cost us untold billions. Not resolving the nation's issues of race and class has and will cost us so much more.

3

Letter to Mr. Howard Blue

William Russell Ellis, Jr.

Guardsmen Evacuate Refugees from Superdome

Saturday, September 2, 2005

New Orleans (AP) *National Guardsmen helped evacuate the mass of storm refugees from the Superdome on Friday, where thousands were stuck in knee-deep trash and blacked-out, putrid bathrooms. "This was the worst night of my life," one mother said.*

At one point, the evacuation was interrupted briefly when school buses rolled up so some 700 guests and employees from the Hyatt Hotel could move to the head of the evacuation line—much to the amazement of those who had been crammed in the stinking Superdome since Sunday.

"How does this work? They [are] clean, they are dry, they get out ahead of us?" exclaimed Howard Blue, 22, who tried to get in their line.

The National Guard blocked him as other guardsmen helped the well-dressed guests with their luggage.

The 700 had been trapped in the hotel, next to the Superdome, but conditions were considerably cleaner, even without running water, than the unsanitary crush inside the dome. The Hyatt was severely damaged by the storm. Every pane of glass on the riverside wall was blown out.

Mayor Ray Nagin has used the hotel as a base, since it is across the street from City Hall, and there were reports the hotel was cleared with priority to make room for police, firefighters and other officials. National Guard Captain John Pollard called the decision to move the Hyatt people to the head of the line "very poor."

Dear Mr. Blue:

I am writing to commend you. On the fourth day, standing amidst the fear and excrement-filled pus of New Orleans, you stood tall and nailed the question of the next thirty years to the wall of the American Superdome: "How Does This Work?"

I felt your shock and amazement at what was uncovered right before your eyes. You asked the key question. Your question was bent, bold, pissed and critical. When you tested it, forcing the National Guard to stop you, your question became coiled action.

You are probably dangerous.

Those are fighting words; words to fight with. The language does not originate with you, nor does the controlled anger that goes with it. "Hold up," "Wait a minute," "Somebody explain to me," are all well-grounded preludes to your disbelieving question ("You folks are NOT really doing this").

Mr. Blue, who can you possibly be? I can't invent you. The Associated Press reporter says you are twenty-two years old.

If so, you are way ahead of the game. I do know that you are now famous. If you search "Howard Blue" on Google, you'll discover that you are known far and wide for your comments. The story is on web sites and web logs all around the country and the world. You'll also discover that you share your name with the author of a recent book *Words at War* (Scarecrow Press, 2002).

Whoever you are, you maintained the personal weight and calm to inspect, describe, question and act on the outrage in front of you, and, by implication, the larger outrage into which you and your comrades in degradation were sunk and stuck.

I hope the notice you have achieved goes to your head. I hope you suffer the arrogance and energy of youth and start asking questions about (let's call them) "The Works" all over New Orleans, Louisiana, and the United States.

If you don't mind, I would like to suggest a couple of aspects of The Works you might consider for further inspection.

As you saw, big events like Katrina momentarily tear away the nicely shaped sheaths that cover The Works. So, for example, you would have to be a very drunken tourist indeed not to have noticed the poverty tucked just round the corner from the fun of New Orleans. Katrina made the poverty, its location, and its color immediately clear to the whole world.

Big Events also have a way of clarifying our understanding of The Works at work. Check this out:

> Recently a Republican Congressman from Louisiana, one Richard Baker, was quoted in national newspapers, including the Wall Street Journal, as having been overheard telling lobbyists in a private conversation: "We finally cleaned up public housing in New Orleans. We couldn't do it, but God did."
>
> —Tom Huckins
> on the Rhetoricians for Peace listserve,
> September 16, 2005

Why is Congressman Baker talking to lobbyists in Washington, DC about God's role in New Orleans's urban renewal? It's part of The Works.

> The rich man in his castle,
> The poor man at his gate,
> He made them, high or lowly,
> And ordered their estate.
> —Christian Hymn

> So many of the people here, you know, were underprivileged anyway, so this is working very well for them.
> —Barbara Bush,
> upon visiting Katrina refugees
> in the Houston Astrodome,
> September 6, 2005

Congressman Baker's God is going to help get New Orleans's public housing situation into a state that works "very well for" everybody. Get ready for lectures about compassionate conservatism, the Christian duty to care for the displaced and destitute. Watch the faith-based funds flow God's way to the trailers where the refugees will need some comfort and explaining to about why their addresses and the city of New Orleans have both been changed permanently and irreconcilably by God and Man.

Something tells me you are going to be an active questioner. But I don't know where The Works will deposit you. If you can, find a way to get over to Punta Gorda, Florida. That will tell you something about what The Works may be processing for your city. God has also gotten into some real estate issues over there.

In the middle of 2004, Hurricane Charley hit Punta Gorda and destroyed most of the small houses and almost all of the public housing. 1500 of those folks were sent to live in 500 trailers in the middle of nowhere. A year later, things are so messed up that a fence surrounds the scene, cops control the one gate in and out, rampant drugs and violence are normal.

As far as I can tell, God has forsaken this place the people now call FEMA City, but has smiled on the town of Punta Gorda:

> . . . (L)andlords found that they could substantially increase their rents in the very tight market . . . "You almost hate to say this because of the difficulties so many people have had, but Charley tore down some buildings that needed to come down and cleared areas for much higher kinds of uses," City Manager Howard Kunic said.
>
> —Marc Kaufman, *Washington Post*, September 17, 2005

"Buildings that needed to come down." Makes Charley sound kinda like God, doesn't it, Mr. Blue? Listen carefully and question when you hear the people in charge talk about "higher kinds of uses" or "highest and best" uses. This usually means that the clean, the dry and the well-fed will move to the head of the line, with God's blessings.

I now realize that I have leapt into this letter expressing no sympathy for you and those around you at the Superdome who shared this hellish experience with you. Clearly it will be an emotional scar for all of you for some time to come. I guess I've assumed that your youth in particular, Mr. Blue, combined with that experience, will send you back into the world with some determination to keep things from "working" again the way they did at that Hyatt moment. I've taken your resilience for granted, based on what you said at the time.

I wish you love, tenderness and deep understanding of your soft and vulnerable side, but I don't want to talk to it as much as to your bent, pissed and dangerous side. I hope the "how does this work?" Howard Blue lives forever and always tries to get in line. Another ordinary thing highlighted by Katrina causes me to take this attitude.

President G. W. Bush has said that he "does not do nuance."

Pressed, he might own up to that being a limit, not a preference.

For sure, he would have been stretched out on a mid-term exam at Yale if asked to explain what Mr. Blue meant by "how does this work"?

But Bush was taught by his Mama Bush to be clear on who ought to stand where in line. There's a moment in Michael Moore's film on him where our president is shown puffed with power, declaring to one of the world's most affluent audiences, "You are my base; the haves and the have mores." (Big, understanding laughter)

That was a twist on the poet Walt Whitman's heartfelt contrast of the haves and have-nots. So, Blue, think with me now about one among several situations in New Orleans. Let's look at the haves and those who have just lost everything, including, almost, hope. Let's go back to a moment and place at the Convention Center when the big Katrina event showed us—in miniature and horribly condensed—"how it works."

A little over a mile from your growing agony, someone named "Bigfoot" called in his account of events unfolding at the Ernest N. Morial Convention Center. Evidently a bar manager and DJ on Bourbon Street, this New Orleans native used his cell phone to call in a version of the report partially summarized below. His account starts from the Iberville Projects where he rode out the brunt of the storm:

> Three days ago, police and national guard troops told citizens to head toward the Crescent City Connection Bridge to await transportation out of the area. The citizens trekked over to the Convention Center and waited for the buses which they were told would take them to Houston or Alabama or somewhere else, out of this area.
>
> It's been three days, and the buses have yet to appear.
>
> . . . There are many infants and elderly people among them, as well as many people who were injured jumping out of windows to escape flood water and the like—all of them in dire straits. Any attempt to flag down police results in being told to get away at gunpoint. Hour after hour they watch buses pass by filled with people from other areas . . .

> **The people are so desperate that they're doing anything they can think of to impress the authorities enough to bring some buses. These things include standing in single file lines with the elderly in front, women and children next; sweeping up the area and cleaning the windows and anything else that would show the people are not barbarians.**
>
> **The buses never stop.**
>
> —www.livejournal.com/users/interdictor/2005/09/01,
> 10:46 PM, emphasis added)

Mr. Blue, despite the horrors the Iberville refugees experienced over those five days, I wonder if you can see in this scene a condensation of what happens in The Big Works! Can you see what happens in the Iberville Projects every day all over the United States? People lining up to get in line to catch the buses that never stop.

Rush up and ask some questions, Mr. Blue, or God's Urban Renewal buses may indeed arrive. They won't be on a road to salvation, but to Negro Removal City.

That's how it wants to work.

Yours, Russ Ellis

4

Making Sense of Tragedy

Rachel E. Luft

So, you've never evacuated from a natural disaster before, and don't know what it's like. You ran into an old acquaintance at the supermarket, and her cousin was there, the one who had been living in New Orleans and that's what you told her, you can't even imagine what she's going through, you thought this was the kind of thing that happened to other kinds of people. You've never gone to sleep your first night in a new apartment without a bed, a couch, towels, or a can opener. You've never had a neighbor email you to tell you that a tree had crashed through your roof, never lost every handpicked picture frame, the ceramic lamp your mother gave you on your sweet sixteenth birthday, the letter from your friend Pat who died the year before, the brand new bottle of face cream you never even opened, the bulging folder of medical records from so many different doctors over the years it was the only complete history of your health that there was. You can't get your mind for one second around the experience of being unable to find your family members. You tell the woman in the supermarket that you recently experienced a relationship breakup, so you do have a sense of what she must be feeling, and also there was that time you moved and everything was in disarray for months.

But you did see the pictures on television, and they were as confusing as they were painful. People staggering around in shock, mostly dark people, clutching children, showing the signs of relentless heat exposure, their surroundings surreal and violent: rooftops torn off, evil water up to the throat, immense Southern oaks tangled with power lines lying across roads and buildings, fires burning on water, men in and out of uniform walking with guns. This can't be America. You've seen pictures like this before and always felt a pang, but it was all so generic, each faraway crisis bleeding into the next, ultimately indistinguishable, and each time you'd find yourself remembering that the people you were seeing were so poor to start out with, they were used to loss, didn't have the luxury of being attached to material things, know how to deal with inconvenience and with suffering. But these pictures are of America, are from the city you actually visited one spring in college where you partied so hard you thought it was Disneyland for adults, and the people staggering on TV speak English, and send their children to school, and have cable and cell phones. It's the undeniable and yet incomprehensible fact that this is happening in America that is so confusing. How can nature be unstoppable in America? How can neither governmental officials nor police know what is happening, not be able to communicate with each other? How could it be even the slightest bit true that they had been warned of these very outcomes and not sent the proper monies down the proper channels to prevent the preventable? How can people huddle on freeway overpasses under road signs marked with the number of an interstate you've actually driven on, surrounded by sewage water in 105° heat index and spend all day and all night and all the next day and all the next night without being picked up by any of the helicopters or boats or Humvees that you can hear in the distance on the news? It's so confusing because if this is happening in America it could happen to you or your grandmother or your children.

As the days go by, you continue to show up for work and pick up the kids and swing by your favorite coffee shop, and still the news keeps coming, the waters keep rising, and it becomes more and more clear that it's not going to be put back together by the weekend. You go about your business because what else can you do, but you are unsettled and distracted, and you swing back and forth between the awareness that you are related to these staggering people, that you have more in common with them than any victims you have ever seen before, and the recurring sense that despite the fact of their Americanness and those recognizable interstate signs and the cell phones in their hands, the truth is that they are still so very different from you. You can see their difference and you can feel it in your gut.

First there's the matter of what they're doing living there at all. Everyone knows the city is twenty feet below sea level. Anyone who moved there made an informed decision, and knew what they were getting into. It's different where you live, in California, where someone is always worried about The Big One, but you've experienced your share of earthquakes and know how harmless they are. Or in the Midwest, where you live, because you've already decided that the next house you're going to buy is going to have a basement you'll use as a tornado shelter, and you're resourceful so you're going to stock it with water and canned goods and your old comfortable couch. Or in the Northwest, where you live, and all the apocalyptic locals and the complaining scientists and the hippy environmentalists are obsessed with the Supervolcano in Yellowstone, but you know that if it were really going to blow the officials simply wouldn't let you live there anymore.

Second, you can't help but return to the thought that those people on the overpass could have saved themselves and so many others a lot of trouble if they had just left with everyone else. It was sheer foolishness—or worse, stubbornness or selfishness—not to. Even you, being so many miles away, heard about Katrina two days before it hit. If you had been there you would have gotten out the Saturday afternoon before the Monday morning landfall, with the rest of the reasonable people. If you had lived there your whole life and heard evacuation warnings one, two, three times a year as long as you could remember, you would have known that this hurricane was going to be different. If you had been living in New Orleans for years, you and your friends would have teased each other anytime one of you actually piled into the car to heed an evacuation recommendation, and when someone who had left drove by your house on their way back into town and passed you sitting comfortably on your front porch you would ask with a grin if they had enjoyed doing the Hurricane Hustle. You would recall that almost a year ago to the day, you and tens of thousands of your neighbors who don't usually leave did evacuate from Hurricane Ivan, and that you spent twelve hours in traffic driving the hundred and eighty-six miles to Jackson, coming home three days later to find no sign of a storm but some leaves on the ground and your garbage can knocked over, but you would realize that this time it would be worth each of those hours on the highway because Katrina was going to be different. On Saturday afternoon you would have packed the important papers, loaded the box of photo albums, filled up with gas and water, and driven north, west, anywhere. You have distant relatives in Atlanta and know you could have stayed with them. Or you'd have gotten a hotel reservation in Memphis and finally taken the family to Graceland. You can't stand it when you overhear people saying that the ones who stayed didn't have any money. You know that there is always enough money if your life is on the line. You're hearing that New Orleans has notoriously low residential turnover, so that a significant proportion of the population has only ever lived in New Orleans, and most of the people they know have only ever lived in New Orleans, but you also know that even if you'd never been out of the city, and if every single person you'd ever met lived in the city, that you would have made reservations at any hotel, anywhere. And if you didn't have credit cards anymore because you'd been living on them for a while a time back and had bad credit and couldn't reserve a hotel room by phone, you would have driven until you ran out of gas and slept in your car. And if you didn't have a car but knew that the hurricane was coming you would have collected up your children and walked on out of there. Watching TV, you had been mesmerized by the 145-MPH winds and the rooftops flying across the city, but you know you would have been able to walk your way out because you would have started on Saturday afternoon the very first hour after hearing that the storm was coming.

And finally, you know such a disaster could never actually have happened to you because you can tell by looking at the TV photos that the people on the overpass were so poor to begin with. You can tell by their hair and the way they speak. You realize that these people were so poor to start out with, they weren't well organized, and this probably got in the way of their common sense. They didn't leave because they're poor and not well organized. You can tell by looking that the people on the overpass are used to loss, don't have the luxury of being attached to material things, know how to deal with inconvenience and with suffering. You realize that this tragedy didn't have to happen if people had just done the right thing, but also that in its own way, it was actually inevitable.

When you get a call from someone from your church asking if you want to pitch in to help several Katrina families find a new home and some furniture, you ask if the church is also going to be helping the local homeless in your city. It doesn't make sense to find the people from the overpass housing if no one is going to do it for the people who sleep in the park in your very own city, and so you tell the person from your church that you won't be joining in the effort, but you hope that someone at the church doesn't forget about the local homeless people. As the days go on you read about people renting apartments in Dallas and in Portland and in Boulder, and it occurs to you that things ultimately turn out for the best, because you'd heard the schools were bad in New Orleans and now the kids who didn't ask for any of this will have a chance. People were given one-way tickets to cities where they didn't know a lot of people, and while this might be a hard adjustment at first, it will surely help break those cycles of poverty. You still have the pang in your gut but the confusion is fading, and it's reassuring to realize that things work out the way they're supposed to, not just for you but for other people too.

5

Will The Circle Be Unbroken?

Reflections on place, identity, and New Orleans culture in the aftermath of Hurricane Katrina

William Sakamoto White

On Friday, August 26, 2005, I had just completed my last class of the day—"The City," a lower-division course that I use to explore New Orleans from an urban sociological foundation. We had just completed a discussion on two articles the students had read during the first week of class—Anthony Orum's article "The Centrality of Place" and Norton Long's "Community of Transients." Our focus was New Orleans, and we discussed how a city like New Orleans, with its various neighborhoods and deep cultural traditions, helped solidify for many of us the "meanings" attached to "place." Did New Orleans hold such "value" for us that, as Long put it, "residents would actually struggle to find the means to remain"? Little did I know then that both of those articles would shape my very thoughts over the coming weeks.

I got home around two PM that afternoon and began my "Friday" ritual—getting my twenty-month-old son Devin ready for our "special" Friday walks through the French Quarter. We start at Decatur Street and Esplanade Avenue and follow the same path with some deviations. We began by saying hello to Miss Kathleen, an antique dealer on Decatur Street, and after gushing over how big Devin continues to get, Kathleen discussed plans for the hurricane evacuation if this was the "big one." Katrina certainly looked impending, but I still had faith that it was going to track to the north after it hit Florida and would move towards the Florida panhandle. With New Orleans safely to the west of the storm, we might enjoy a wonderful, humidity-free few days after the storm made landfall in Florida. Kathleen informed us that she was taking refuge in her apartment on the second story of a building in the Marigny and as long as her family was safe she could ride this one out. I haven't heard from Kathleen since and I hope she didn't ride it out—but I also wonder, whether she survived the storm or not, if I will ever see her again.

Devin and I continue on our stroll through the Quarter. I stop for a quick Sangria to go at Mojo's café where Devin loves to torment the owners' new kitten, Nola. Nola is freely roaming the bar, and it's probably illegal for both Devin and the cat to be there anyway, but they all love Devin and as long as he's in the stroller, he can come inside with me. With drink in hand, we continue our journey down Decatur Street. We say hello to Maybeth and Rhonda at Funrockin', two dear friends who shower my children with affection and way too many sugar treats.

Part of our Friday ritual is to head towards the Mississippi River along the Riverwalk. "Old Man River" is a bit busy with barges moving up river, large tankers heading down, the Canal Street Ferries working their way from Algiers to Canal Street, and all the activity that makes the River so picturesque. The history, the culture, the stories that come from the River— I tell Devin that our walk here is our way of paying respect for this incredible natural feature we are so privileged to live next to.

As we head back into Jackson Square, we hear the musicians and grab another drink to go at Harry's Corner. We say hello to various friends that line Chartres, Royal, and Decatur Streets and then head home to tell Mommy about our adventures. Once home, I wander to the computer and examine the latest reports on Katrina. It has not taken that northern turn like people had anticipated. The computer models now show that it's heading straight for New Orleans and it will intensify. I know we have time to get things in order and there is no reason to panic. I walk around the house and measure things up on what we can pack and what we can leave behind. The ritual of evacuation begins, and though we probably do this twice a year, I know that if this one hits New Orleans, there won't be much left of the city. This would be the last walk through the French Quarter I would have with my son Devin.

Orum (1997) writes that the most concrete manner in which place presents itself to us is in the form of neighborhoods. Neighborhood is the place where we grew up, where we developed our friendships, where we went to school, where many of our parents may have worked, and what we remember best. Neighborhoods represent a physical place where we regenerate all the stored memories and meanings of place. My centrality of place is both where I live in the Broadmoor neighborhood and where I travel in the French Quarter. I have developed relationships in the Quarter like those that Long describes as "friendships from shared common goods—friendships of pleasure and of commerce and, at the highest level, friendships developed in the pursuit of some significant vision of the good life" (1991:6). Over the years, I have become a Quarter Character, a person recognizable as I pass along its streets. Street musicians, shop owners, bartenders, and street people know me, and we share in conversations and happenings. I am recognized as a DJ at WWOZ and as the guy who wears quirky shirts, straw hats, and is always pushing a stroller with Devin everywhere I go.

I make a point to visit as many people as I can when I go for those walks, and we share a common bond of the "vision" of New Orleans—a culture of "carefreeness" that doesn't exist in any other city.

New Orleans is a city where the culture emerges from the interaction of history, social forces, and the neighborhoods. Jazz, for example, can only emerge in a city like New Orleans— the history influences it, with a unique and special "tiered" society that rewarded mixed-blood Creole offspring with "middle-man" status and marginality (Hall, 1992). The Creole were historically the "second tier" of New Orleans society. They could go to school, play brass and string instruments, read sheet music, and play in bands. They could even own property and businesses. The "third tier" was held by the African slaves who the governing French and Spanish elites allowed to freely roam the streets of the city on Sundays. For African slaves, this allowed them to practice the rituals, customs, and participate in social institutions they could remember from Africa. No place better exemplifies how slaves were able to maintain their cultural roots than Congo Square, where they practiced the rhythmic "bamboula" beats of Africa and celebrated their customs. At the end of the nineteenth century, Americans had completely taken over the government structure of the city. Creoles found themselves lumped with the descendants of slaves into a new conglomerated "second-tier" Black society. Creoles and Blacks began to teach each other their own customs and rituals. Classically trained Creole musicians and Blacks who maintained their cultural ties to African rhythms merged the sounds into what we call "jazz" today. Without this history, jazz would not exist. A new culture emerged from this initial mix of experiences of the African diaspora. I wonder what culture will emerge from the new post-Katrina diaspora in the cities the evacuees find themselves in.

The Mardi Gras Indians, a Black working-class neighborhood-based social and cultural institution, provide another key example of New Orleans culture born from the interaction between Creoles, Blacks, and segregation. The Mardi Gras Indians began at the turn of the century as a reaction to Blacks being denied the opportunity to celebrate Mardi Gras. Their distinctive costumes and musical chants embody much of the interaction between music and neighborhood that New Orleans is famous for. Taking their makebelieve identities from a historical relationship between escaped slaves and the Native Americans who protected them, Tribe members are ranked, with the "Big Chief" maintaining the leadership position. Members work on their costumes all year long, putting countless hours and many dollars into the completed outfit. The "battles" these tribes engage in are based on the beauty of Big Chiefs' costumes as they measure each other up when tribes confront each other on the streets. The one with the most beautiful costume is the one who is recognized as the "best" chief. For many who have not experienced viewing the Mardi Gras Indians on Mardi Gras day or St. Joseph's night, this may seem like a fruitless endeavor. For those of us who understand the culture of New Orleans, it is a ritual and spectacle to be revered and honored. In the post-Hurricane diaspora, with many of these Mardi Gras Indians separated from their communities and fellow members, we could anticipate that this tradition, though perhaps to be mimicked in the years to come, won't be true or real.

On Sunday, August 28, my family, my next-door neighbor Miss Lee and my friend Melissa got into two cars and left New Orleans. Earlier Saturday night, my wife Susan and I went to pick up Melissa at her apartment in the Marigny. We traveled down Royal Street in the French Quarter and noticed the neighborhood looking very "normal." Though there were a number of businesses which had boarded up, tourists were walking down the street, bars were open, and musicians were playing on the sidewalks. I told Susan and Melissa that this might be the last time we see the French Quarter. I could see Susan's eyes water. She knew this might be true.

It was early morning when we left for Lafayette. Susan and I knew this could be our last time viewing the house in its current condition. We had just completed painting our bedroom this spring with burgundy walls, a dark blue ceiling with gold stars on it, bordered with white crown molding—colors and styles that only a New Orleanian would understand and appreciate. Each room in our house was colorful this way and the art in the house reflected our funky, eclectic, "New Orleans" interpretation. As she turned away from the front door, Susan began to cry.

My family and I have now "settled" into a small, rural, nearly all-white town in Tennessee near Knoxville. Devin has adjusted very well, almost as if nothing had happened. Susan and I know that what happens to us in the meantime is the story of many middle-, working- and lower-income evacuees in New Orleans—we must choose between survival in the communities we have relocated to or coming back home, encouraged by the polices New Orleans has implemented. I have been back to New Orleans once since the storm and found our house full of mold, our furniture destroyed, and the house showing other signs of damage from having two feet of contaminated water inside of it. Our centrality of place has been significantly disturbed, and we have had to "compromise" our lives once again. New Orleans was not a compromise for us—socially, culturally, or racially. It was a city that held for us a number of meanings that were attached to place.

The question for us now is not necessarily what Long (1991) considers the desire to fight for such a valuable place by remaining and struggling to save it. The key, says Long, is to "remain." Hurricanes force people to "leave." The challenge for us is to either recreate new centralities of place in our new communities, or to find the means to return to New Orleans and reestablish the rich culture that made New Orleans the place we loved so much. I'm not sure that either goal can be achieved. I see a very different New Orleans emerging in the future—one that will lose the rich culture of its past and create for itself a new culture based on the new communities and new residents. The city will still be on the map, but it will not be the same. And, unfortunately, Susan, Devin and I may find compromise again a significant part of our life.

In these weeks since we've left New Orleans, I still take my Friday afternoon walks with Devin, driving an hour into Knoxville so we can stroll downtown in Market Square and the Old City neighborhood. The music we hear isn't jazz, and the sights and scents are still unfamiliar. But, for now, this is as close as we can get to the feeling of New Orleans. As he grows up, we'll discuss the place where we are and the things we see, but I will also tell him about a great city called New Orleans, and hope these stories will help guide him to find his own centrality of place.

References

Hall, Gwendolyn Midlo. "The Formation of Afro-Creole Culture." In Hirsch, Arnold and Joseph Logsdon (eds.), *Creole New Orleans: Race and Americanization.* Baton Rouge, Louisiana: Louisiana State University Press, 1992.

Long, Norton. "The Paradox of a Community of Transients." *Urban Affairs Quarterly* 27(1):1–12, 1991.

Orum, Anthony. *The Centrality of Place: The Urban Imagination of Sociologists.* Great Cities Institute, College of Urban Planning and Public Affairs, University of Illinois, Chicago, 1997.

6

Displacement, Gentrification and the Politics of Exclusion

Andrew Jolivette

As a descendant of the Creole people of Louisiana, I feel a personal connection to the Hurricane Katrina crisis and its victims. As a sociologist, I am cognizant of why the displaced masses of poor and African-American citizens of New Orleans are referred to by the government and the media as "refugees" and "looters". The value placed on the poor and on people of color in this country has always been based on the ability of dominant classes to subordinate these communities and gentrification is but one manifestation of this structural process of exclusion.

Monday, August 29 was not the beginning of the displacement that New Orleans residents now face in the aftermath of Hurricane Katrina. Gentrification throughout one of America's most historic cities has slowly but steadily taken place over the past several decades. As Kevin Fox Gotham and John Arena at Tulane University (2003) point out, many scholars argue that gentrification is fundamentally different than it was in the 1970s and 1980s. Gotham and Arena point to three major changes in the gentrification process of New Orleans. First, new forms of national and local intervention and entrepreneurial governance have altered the local context of gentrification in New Orleans. They use the concept "neoliberal gentrification" to refer to the role of state devolution, withdrawal and privatization in pressuring local governments to actively pursue redevelopment and gentrification as ways of bolstering the tax base and generating revenue. Second, they look at the "corporatization" of the French Quarter. Third, they point to the increasing marginalization of anti-gentrification movements along race and class lines.

As I sit and watch CNN and Fox News along with the rest of the world, I struggle personally and professionally to grapple with the response to Hurricane Katrina and with the pre-existing state of Louisiana's political and moral responsibility to the poor, elderly, and the disenfranchised populations of New Orleans. There is a long history in this country of race and class divisions. It is usually easier to continue perpetuating these divisions, or to simply pretend they do not exist, than to critically interrogate and dismantle these oppressive systems of domination. Questions like: Why was the response so slow? Should they rebuild New Orleans? Who will rebuild New Orleans? Who will benefit from the rebuilding? are all fundamental to questioning key issues of inequality, race, and white supremacy in the United States.

But more important in this situation is the question of leadership and ethics. Gentrification and poverty have grown in New Orleans as a result of corporate tourism, citizen neglect, and a loss of hope. This hopelessness and poverty left many of the most vulnerable with no viable means to evacuate the city, with no collective leadership responding to their needs and rights as human beings. Cornel West in his bestseller *Race Matters* argues that the loss of hope or "nihilism" is destroying Black communities in this country. He also asserts that without a politics of conversion we would not see an end to the suffering and inequality along this country's racial fault lines.

But nihilism is not overcome by arguments or analyses; it is tamed by love and care. Any disease of the soul must be conquered by a turning of one's soul. This turning is done through one's own affirmation of one's worth—an affirmation fueled by the concern of others. A love ethic must be at the center of any progressive humane politics. While the Mayor, Governor, and President all failed to respond to this crisis in a way that would have prevented the loss of lives and the possibility of renewed gentrification at unparalleled levels once the city is rebuilt, we need to pay close attention to the corporate cultural appropriation taking place in the city of New Orleans.

Known as a city famous for its food, music, and cultural traditions, New Orleans, not unlike Hawaii, has become a place where displacement is common and seen as an inevitable part of the post-industrial moment of the twenty-first century. Until we begin to face the question of race head-on without fear and hesitancy, until we begin to face the painful history and present condition of people of color in this country, we will be doomed to repeat the group conflicts that led to the undemocratic formation of this nation.

7

The Poliatrics of Nueva Orleans

Guillermo Delgado-P.
and Norma Klahn

*El Mississippi es río de pecho ancho; es un infinito
y oscuro hermano del Paraná, del Uruguay, del
Amazonas y del Orinoco.*[1]

—Jorge Luis Borges, 1954

"I did not know Nueva Orleans was built under sea level," a friend stated. "I did not realize this when I last visited. I did know, however," our friend continued, "the important role Nueva Orleans played in the context of geopolitics." We became actively engaged in many such dialogues through phone conversation and email exchanges as Katrina and its effects were reported worldwide. As we watched a city and its citizens desperately looking for ways to survive, we learned, as did our international community of friends, about a city we had all visited in 2002, guests of two universities that had opened their doors to Latin Americanists (scholars, writers and artists) for a conference. We all now know that New

[1]The Mississippi is a broad-chested river; it is an infinite and dark brother of the Paraná, of the Uruguay, of the Amazon, and of the Orinoco.

Orleans is under sea level; that located at the mouth of the Mississippi, it is the largest port of the United States by tonnage and America's gateway to the global market. In the geographic spectrum, it has been a center for international trade since 1718, and it competes with the Ports of Miami in Florida, Long Beach in California, Houston in Texas and Veracruz in Mexico. We have now also been made painfully aware of what being under sea level means. It was a surprise and a shock to learn that every system there (health, communications, power lines, water and sewage system, police and fire departments, and government in general) linked with the life of this vibrant city could collapse in a couple of days. Now we could seriously begin to think about *poliatrics.*[2]

Loyola and Tulane Universities in New Orleans held the First International Congress on Bolivian Studies in the year 2002. The memories retained of that event force us, as participants, to pay homage and repeat a never-ending gratitude to these institutions for hosting an academic event of such rarity. There were no precedents because who cares about Bolivia in the world of globalization, or for that matter for the peoples of Chiapas, or the 67% of African Americans living below the poverty line in New Orleans? Today, the very colleagues who welcomed us at Loyola and Tulane are now dispersed, along with so many other evacuees who survived. So it is with pain that we recall great moments of sharing and camaraderie as we talked about our research and explored the very "soul" of New Orleans.

In Loyola and Tulane we found a space where the exchange of ideas became a space of reciprocity from where to think socially transformative projects. Loyola and Tulane had offered the small group of academicians, interested in Latin America's pressing social issues, the opportunity of subsequently hosting a Web page that would contribute to

---

[2]Héctor Abad Morales coined this term in his article "Public Health Problems in Medellín." The term refers to: "The treatment of the diseases of the city or state" in M. Edel and R. G. Hellman, eds. *Cities in Crisis* (New York: Bildner Center for Western Hemisphere Studies, 1989), 103.

enhancing mutual understanding and collaboration between developed and developing societies. For the time being, one now appreciates the enormous role played by both universities in lending us a hand to enhance communication and promote human empathy in today's interactive world. Due to obvious reasons, the web page, a victim of nature as well, is down. Presumably it will come back, and hopefully, soon. This hope also goes for the whole city and its people.

The collapse of the city had been prophesied for years. John McQuid and Mark Schleifstein, reporters at the *Times-Picayune*, which continued to issue the daily on the internet despite Katrina, had predicted the devastating possibilities in 2002. No one listened to the warning that the New Orleans levees needed strengthening if the city was to withstand a major storm. Being an urban complex under sea level, surrounded by levees, these simply gave up at the first sign of an overwhelming natural push. Although scientists had pointed out the fragility of such retainers, their reinforcement was not part of the official agenda. And indeed, as stated by the writer Darryl Pinckney, "something of the deep racism in US society has been exposed inadvertently—to an international audience," being that the overflowing occurred largely in the poorest neighborhoods in New Orleans with a majority African-American population.[3]

From the perspective of, among others, Haiti, Nicaragua, Bolivia or Southern Mexico—where, whether in rural or urban settings, economic poverty lingers—the images of New Orleans that started to hit the TV screens brought to the front unimaginable depictions. Viewers could not fathom that in the richest country in the world citizens could be so marginalized and then, given the catastrophe, treated with what appeared at times as indifference, negligence and even contemptuous disrespect. The not-so-accessible history of Afro-American culture in other parts of the world, such as Bolivia, left viewers troubled, with a deeper understanding

---

[3] *The New York Review of Books,* October 6, 2005, 6.

of capitalism's failures as Katrina exhibited concrete poverty and tangible discrimination. Relatives on the Mexican side of the border could not believe the number of citizens so disenfranchised. These scenes, we were told, were changing previous perceptions of the United States as land of plenty and equality.

Given the distance that mediated our dialogues, an imaginary was summoned, and a few names were retrieved and kept being invoked to make sense of a place, and as ways to identify the "who" are we talking about. Names such as the great Louis Armstrong, the Rev. Martin Luther King, Rosa Parks, the term "Jazz," Mardi Gras, Preservation Hall, Betty Winn, Fats Domino, and the Marsalis family were immediately linked to the scene in a composite that mapped a Greater New Orleans—to many, these names represented an Americas *Geist*. Mexicans call it 'the third root,' contributions of an entire African people to the meaning of the Americas, not just the United States. This tribute did not fade the images coming through, or the solidarity with the lament voiced by African Americans from all walks of life, who couldn't believe that the apparatus failed its people in such a flagrant way. The *New Yorker* columnist Nicolas Lemann wrote that "There was no obvious person in charge, and no obvious plan being carried out."[4] Belatedly, Louisiana political representatives in the US Congress also expressed this same sentiment.

For Mexican friends watching, it was a reminder of how the earthquake of September 19, 1985 had made apparent not only the devastations nature can bring upon a community, but of a similar state negligence that made greater the loss and pain. We remembered that in Mexico, from the ruins of the devastated city, an invisible part of the population, an ignored sector of society, became visible to the eyes of the world. Thousands then lost their lives or what little they owned. The response of civil society confronted by this tragedy, as in New Orleans, was inspiring in its solidarity with its survivors,

---

[4] *The New Yorker*, September 12, 2005, 34.

forming in the aftermath rescue teams, while the Federal government's inactivity and slowness to react brought to the fore questions of the role of the state's responsibilities to its citizens. For a Bolivian peasant watching the news all this was absolutely appalling; it didn't add up. From Luis Ernesto Derbez, the Mexican Secretary of Foreign Affairs, we learned that 40,000 undocumented Mexican workers, another invisible population, were also stranded in Nueva Orleans.[5] Katrina implicitly posed the unanswered questions of globalization and the need for agreements on international human rights.

It was only natural, that while watching events unfolding during the last days of August and the first ones of September of 2005, we tried to locate and follow friends and colleagues by now inevitably affected. On the phone Urbano Choque asked: "Are you close to that city?" Our response that we lived in California, and far from Louisiana, was only half comforting, as he again inquired, "But our friend Josefa lives there, right there, doesn't she?" We had not yet heard from her at this time. Two weeks later, when we finally located Josefa, she let us know that she and many others had lost, and this is not a metaphor, *everything:* manuscripts that represented months of research, archival materials, book collections that collapsed along with soaked shelves; and the mementos that narrate one's journey through life, pictures, documents and the many accumulated belongings of value not easily appraised and impossible to retrieve or replace. A professor of the Modern Foreign Languages and Literature Department at Loyola University, Josefa Salmón also informed us that the university was "locked and double locked," safeguarded to protect the infrastructure of the campus. It seemed the most reasonable thing to do, given the situation. Yet the idea of a gated university makes us think twice. Our hope is that the protective fences will be removed soon so that the

---

[5]Andrea Becerril, "Señala Derbez que son más de 100 mil los mexicanos afectados por Katrina," *La Jornada,* September 1, 2005

university can continue its pedagogical mission cultivating, in addition, the new knowledges that Katrina has brought to the surface.

The news is long gone, but the "real" problems remain. "The city," reports Gary Rivlin, "has laid off half its workforce, and the state university is preparing for thousands of layoffs . . ."[6] It may be a while before the New Orleans we knew is back. We all hope that in future urban planning the inequality that surfaced will be addressed, and that a safe environment, adequate housing, health services, schooling, and equal access to jobs become available to all its citizens. As the city reconstitutes itself both structurally and socially, it can serve as a model for other cityscapes, most of which are not exempt from the issues brought up by Katrina.

---

[6] *The New York Times*, October 2, 2005, 1.

Loss of Heritage,
Discovery of Injustice:
Elders and Premature Babies

Andrea Steiner

The news coverage of Hurricane Katrina featured a soundtrack
that no other tragedy will ever muster. New Orleans always
had the best music. At some gut level this was the first loss
to pierce the American perception—the destruction of the
music scene, and our immediate nostalgia for the heady,
erotic French Quarter and its Mardi Gras celebrations. Next
came the visuals, and now it was clear to the world that the
human losses were not solely due to accident after all; they
were preponderantly and disproportionately poor Black
people, living on lower ground, without transportation or the
funds to get out quickly. I watched and read, with everyone
else, and then I noticed something: Nobody was writing
about the old people.

Who was most likely to die? After the casualties of falling
telephone poles and crashing roofs, it would have to be people
who could not get out. Caught up in the water and then the
110° heat, it would be hospital patients, prison inmates, the

residents of nursing homes. People without transportation. Those who were slow. Those who just couldn't take another great change in their lives. To a large extent, it would be the elders.

It was five days before the public eye even noticed, five days of silence and invisibility followed by shock/horror reportage and official-sounding rationalizations of the inequalities and lost histories made plain on our television sets. The shock and horror are real; St. Rita's Nursing Home, with its thirty-four wheelchair-bound residents huddled at the door, no doubt clamoring for help or an exit, will forever be an icon of that. We now know that many people in Louisiana's for-profit hospitals and nursing homes escaped the hurricane, evacuated in privately hired helicopters. Public care facilities, however, had contracted with the same small bus company—fine when one building has a fire or burst pipes, but wholly inadequate when every place in the city needs that same minivan now. In terms of evacuation, the elders living on their own were in the same boat as the rest of their neighbors, although probably many had a relatively greater need. That greater need never translated into a higher spot on the evacuators' priority list.

In fact, elders were rationalized as deserving a low place on that list. These rationalizations are offensive, all the worse for their illegitimate sense of legitimacy. I was watching the morning news one Saturday after Katrina struck, and jerked to attention when the reporter referred to the rising number of deaths "attributable" to Katrina. "They're leaving out the old people," I muttered to myself. And indeed that was the case. According to the *New York Times*, the Louisiana State Department of Health and Hospitals is not sure what's fair when it comes to counting the dead. The coroner's operations officer from East Baton Rouge Parish commented that most "were either elderly . . . or premature babies . . ." and then added the kicker: "I'm hesitant to count those as storm-related."

Not storm-related? Aging reduces the body's ability to maintain its balance, called homeostatic function, and to regain it after a knock. Elders come back to 'normal' more slowly than the young. The severity of the flooding was nothing if not a knock, and older bodies were vulnerable during that slower return to physiological balance. Eighty-two percent of Americans aged 65+ have at least one chronic disease to manage, such as diabetes or hypertension, and seventy percent of those aged 80+ have five or more.[1] They rely on daily medication or specialized equipment. In New Orleans, older people with chronic illnesses were not damaged by their conditions so much as by being separated from these supports. And there is more. In late life, severe trauma or change can catapult a person into a delirium that looks a lot like dementia. In such a state of profound disorientation, simply taking care of yourself—not to mention your house—falls by the wayside. As for the premature babies, to a significant degree that is code for lack of prenatal care, which in turn is code for access problems, which all too often mean inadequate health insurance or unavailable, inappropriate services. In urgent circumstances—like a category 5 hurricane—babies often come "prematurely."

With all possible respect, the coroner's office was saying that old people don't count, and neither do the babies of poor women. There is an economic incentive to assert these exclusions, in that FEMA is meant to pay for disaster-related funerals, but that is not sufficient to excuse this policy-in-the-making.

The government has said it wants to help all the Katrina victims, but little aid is forthcoming. Congress is bickering

---

[1] In a September 12 email, the US Administration on Aging reported to state Departments of Aging that five percent of New Orleans's 17,000 evacuees in Houston's Convention Center were aged 60+. The memo continued, "Anecdotal information shared with us indicates that many seniors have not accepted the fact that they do not have a home to return too [*sic*], and are suffering from relocation trauma. It was also noted that many low income seniors are caring for their grandchildren in the shelter." [new paragraph] "Thank you very much, and have a nice weekend!"

over Medicaid waiver policies while people of all ages are stranded without medicine and care; some forty-six percent of those seeking coverage are being turned away. Regarding the elderly, the Federal Administration on Aging reports that its budget is "fully committed." Instead of issuing resources, it provided a list of things evacuees need and charities that will accept donations. What an appalling failure of political will that is. In California, the Department of Aging announced that it had added a "Katrina Question and Answer" section to the CDA Web site; searching there two weeks later, I found no link. In the meantime, reports from the field describe a great deal of emotional shock, associated maladjustment, and tremendous physical risk. The elderly are again in the forefront of anticipated deaths, whether ultimately defined as "attributable" or not.

If ever a case could be made that solidarity among the invisible and devalued of America was warranted, that time would be now. Yet, stepping back from Katrina for a moment, too many senior advocacy organizations have circled their wagons and focused on protecting their threatened services. This may be understandable, but it misses the opportunity for elders to lead or at least share in the fight for universal policies that would protect all people and promote our collective social welfare. Too many child/youth advocacy organizations have raised awareness of their constituents' vulnerability by comparing their terrible economic status (without benefits) to the better-off status of seniors (largely because of benefits). It is time to end this competitive advocacy, and instead to work across class, color, and generations for a common cause.

To borrow a British expression, today New Orleans is at the coal face; metaphorically, we are standing with the men who are down in the mines. At the coal face, we confront the loss of a rich heritage, and grieve. We find elders and premature babies, abandoned by infrastructure, institutions, and social assumptions. We find, if we are looking, a chance to reckon with these injustices. Perhaps now we can do more than rebuild the world. Perhaps we can reconstruct it.

References

Barringer, F. and D. G. McNeil Jr. "Storm and crisis: the hospitals; grim triage for ailing and dying at a makeshift airport hospital." *The New York Times*, September 3, 2005.

CBS Morning News. September 24, 2005.

Connolly, L. Email from Acting Director of California Department of Aging to "interested parties," September 7, 2005.

Damon, N. Email from California Department of Aging to "interested parties," September 16, 2005.

Dewan, S. "Storm and crisis: the dead; often, tolls don't show true picture." *The New York Times*, September 22, 2005.

Gross, J. "When crisis strikes, an orderly exit?" *The New York Times*, September 22, 2005.

Smith, V. and M. Ritter. "Catastrophe hits elderly the hardest." *The Indianapolis Star*, September 8, 2005.

www.dailykos.com/story/2005/9/4/11430/17556. Daily Kos: Nursing Homes Underwater. 9 pages, posted September 3, 2005 at 22:14:30 PDT.

Rohde, D., D. G. McNeil Jr., R. Abelson, and S. Dewan. "Storm and crisis; the victims; vulnerable and doomed in the storm." *The New York Times*, September 19, 2005.

Rovner, J. "Bush debates health care for Katrina victims." Reported on National Public Radio's Morning Edition, September 30, 2005.

Wolff, J. L., B. Starfield, and G. Anderson. "Prevalence, expenditures, and complications of multiple chronic conditions in the elderly." *Archives of Internal Medicine*, 2002; 162:2269-2276.

US Administration on Aging, September 12 email to state Departments on Aging, forwarded to directors of Area Agencies on Aging.

www.partnershipforsolutions.org/program. "The problem: about chronic conditions." Partnership for Solutions, July 24, 2002.

New Orleans Is All of Us

David Anthony

New Orleans is all of us. A generation ago, in 1971, the Attica Correctional Facility in New York State became infamous for the manner in which then-Governor Nelson A. Rockefeller, and the state apparatus he controlled, overreacted to what began as a demonstration to improve conditions within the prison. The Governor ordered state police and the National Guard to suppress the revolt using deadly force, in effect declaring martial law against the protesting rebels. The vast majority of those incarcerated in Attica were men of color, principally African-American, Latino, Native American, but it contained a critical mass of poor whites as well. The uprising was covered in full view of the news media, print, television and radio. Attica became a source of not only local, but regional and very soon afterward, national attention, once negotiations began to break down because the insurrectionists had seized hostages. After a tense period during which the inmates felt that they had been treated unfairly, the governor and his allies laid siege to the prison, "restoring order" in a hail of bullets that contributed to the conditions in which many of the hostages were killed, as well as several of the leaders of the action. In the aftermath of the lethal confrontation a riot commission was assembled to examine the causes of the protest and to assess how it was handled. Defenders of the rights of the prisoners to rise up and demand their democratic privileges began to express their solidarity with them using the slogan *Attica is all of us.*

One should not take the analogy too far, since New Orleans should not be seen as a correctional facility—though many portrayed the embattled Ninth Ward as if it were an annex to a prison. But there are certain disturbing parallels in the ways in which the horrific destruction of Hurricane Katrina became a symbol of everything that the powerful saw as wrong with New Orleans. And what was "wrong" was increasingly seen as the city's large underclass—which coincidentally also happened to share the "racial" characteristics of the majority of the inmates of Attica and virtually every major correctional institution in the United States.[1] In that sense, the inner city and the prison are not that far apart; anyone who has resided, worked or spent any significant amount of time in the former has absolutely no illusions about its organic connection to the latter. Thus it was only a matter of time before looting and other ostensible manifestations of criminality became the focal point of establishment news reportage. At the same time, however, there was also a counter-narrative of human response to a catastrophe of cataclysmic dimensions, a deluge of seemingly Biblical force, whose enormity compelled thinking and feeling folk to strive to transcend racial blinders. This counter-narrative could be glimpsed in the independent, progressive press and in the heroic tales related by survivors among themselves and any outsiders they risked trusting.

The contradiction between the scandalous slandering of

---

[1] Editor's note: Published reports of meetings of the New Orleans business/political elite shows them to be interested in a "new demographics" for a rebuilt city in which there will be "fewer people"—read that to mean a kind of ethnic cleansing to rid the city of the Black working class. See also the essay by Hardy Frye in this book.

a population already rendered numb by the devastation of the disaster, and the projection of race and racial prerogatives upon a situation where everyone, high and low, Black, white and every hue in between suffered a level of victimization with which sentient human beings should have been able to identify, made it difficult for the counter-narrative to be heard, and if uttered, to be taken seriously. When a disaster occurs it does not matter how much foreknowledge the authorities had of it. In human terms it is actually quite irrelevant that New Orleans had been sinking into the sea for a century or more, for everyone knew that it was situated below sea level.

It is not that warnings were disregarded with clearly and unprecedentedly tragic consequences. Rather it is that, after the evacuation strategy failed, after the recovery process was revealed to be ill-conceived, if not stillborn, and after every single fiber of the bureaucracy had broken down, like everything else that was overrun by the ruthless ravages of the flood tide, then it became time to save those who could be saved, where they were, because they needed saving. Yet the heroic counter-narrative had to contend with the venal decisions of police and others, whose sense of propriety put the maintaining of order over the distribution of those resources that had been marshaled to help relieve the suffering of the masses of the people.

In these circumstances, the exodus that created a nation-wide New Orleanean diaspora, and sparked heated debates over the semantic distinctions between "evacuees" and "refugees," needs to be contextualized in terms of the counter-narrative of survival in the face of seemingly insurmountable odds, where aged and infirm senior citizens clung to rooftops; where homeowners and renters alike risked their lives to protect their pets; and where, in the trenches, all that ultimately mattered was how to help oneself and others stay alive. Those lessons cannot be lost on us. We are still here because we have a purpose in being here, however we choose to name that reason for being. That which causes pain to other human beings should be the source of pain to all of us. Hence our impulse to help should arise out of our innermost desire to express our connectedness to one another. The best of us, throughout the Gulf region, the nation and the world at large all recognized that. For them the fact was abundantly clear: *New Orleans is all of us.*

10

Katrina and Social Justice

Bettina Aptheker

1

A news story datelined Baton Rouge, Louisiana five days after Hurricane Katrina described a group of refugees on Causeway Boulevard in New Orleans who "stood out." They were a six-year-old boy walking down the road, carrying a five-month-old baby, surrounded by five toddlers. The children were holding hands, with the six-year-old clearly in charge. Three of the children were about two years old; and then there was a three-year-old taking care of her fourteen-month-old brother. The six-year-old identified himself as Deamonte Love, and then identified each of the other children. Rescuers brought them to Child Protective Services in Baton Rouge. The children, according to the rescuers, were clean and healthy and well cared for. The news story reported that their mothers, who also had been rescued, had been flown to San Antonio, Texas. They found their children after a frantic search on the internet where a web site posted pictures of lost children and their location. As soon as the mothers' identities were confirmed the children were flown to them.

It turned out that four days after the hurricane the children and their four respective mothers and one of their fathers were still in their apartment complex, with everything flooded and no way out. They were without food, had run out of water, and had no milk for the babies. A rescue helicopter finally landed. The pilot said he had room only for the children, and gave the parents less than a minute to make a decision. Following the advice of the dad "To let the babies go," the mothers agreed. The pilot promised to return for the adults, but he never came back. Making their own way out the parents eventually were airlifted to San Antonio, Texas.

The children were treated very well at the shelter. One of the workers who had cared for them said, "I think what's going to stick with them is that they survived Hurricane Katrina, and that they were loved." This may well be true, and it is also true that both parents and children will long be afflicted with post-traumatic shock. The questions are, what was the helicopter pilot thinking when he dropped the children off alone? And could all of this have been prevented in the first place?

Meanwhile, two weeks after Katrina, an African-American woman named Frances Elaine Newton was executed in Huntsville, Texas for allegedly killing her husband and their two children in April 1987. She was convicted in October 1988. Newton and her family were from Houston. She had steadfastly maintained her innocence over the seventeen years of her incarceration, and was reported by authorities to be a model prisoner. Her court-appointed public defender prepared no defense during her trial. The Houston police failed to investigate that her husband's murder might have been connected to the fact that he was a known drug dealer. A massive political effort to save her life failed, despite the intervention of scores of human and civil rights organizations. Even the American Bar Association urged a stay of execution and a new trial because of its serious concerns about the conduct of the police, and critical errors in the forensic evidence prepared by the Houston crime lab. Appeals to the Texas governor were to no avail.

Ms. Newton's parents Iva Jewel Nelms and Bee Henry Nelms, Jr. witnessed her execution. Iva Nelms vowed to continue in the struggle to prove her daughter's innocence and to then sue the Houston police and Texas prison authorities for false arrest, false imprisonment and murder. Since 1982, when the death penalty was reinstated, there have been 982 executions in the United States; 805 have taken place in the South, 349 of them in the state of Texas alone.

Then, exactly one month after Katrina, William Bennett, the former Secretary of Education under Ronald Reagan and the director of drug control policy under President George H. W. Bush, and an influential consultant to the current President, said on his radio talk show, "Morning in America," that "I do know that it's true that if you wanted to reduce crime, you could, if that were your sole purpose, you could abort every Black baby in this country, and your crime rate would go down." He was responding to a caller who cited a book noting that an increase in the abortion rate had helped reduce the crime rate. Bennett went on to say that such an abortion policy would be "an impossible, ridiculous and morally reprehensible thing to do, but your crime rate would go down." In the subsequent firestorm of protest demanding an apology for his statement, Secretary Bennett blamed the media for distorting what he meant, although he repeatedly reiterated the correlation between Black children and crime rates, and refused to apologize.

The 1949 United Nations Convention on Genocide defines it as killing members of a national, ethnical, racial, or religious group; causing serious bodily or mental harm to members of the group; deliberately inflicting on the group conditions of life calculated to bring about its physical destruction in whole or in part; imposing measures to prevent births within the group; and forcibly transferring children of the group to another group. Secretary Bennett's statements certainly fall within the purview of genocidal incitement. They also completely decimate African-American women's right to bear children in safety and with a full measure of material well-being.

Finally, five weeks after Hurricane Katrina Robert Davis, a sixty-four-year-old African-American retired elementary school teacher was beaten by two New Orleans police officers in the French Quarter, allegedly for "public intoxication." An Associated Press Television News producer, who happened to be on the scene, filmed the episode, and was himself attacked by a third police officer. Mr. Davis said he had returned to New Orleans to check on his property. On Saturday night, October 8, he had gone out to buy cigarettes. He said he hadn't had a drink in twenty-five years. According to Mr. Davis' attorney he was baffled by the incident and did not see it as a "racial thing." The two police officers were arraigned on battery charges, and released pending a January 2006 trial. According to Rachel La Corte, an Associated Press writer, the New Orleans police department has long been plagued by allegations of brutality and corruption.

Between the six-year-old African-American child leading his small band of hurricane survivors in New Orleans, the execution of Frances Elaine Newton in Huntsville, Texas, the "wisdom" of Secretary Bennett, and the beating of Robert Davis, all within five weeks of the hurricane, falls the long and fateful shadow of racism, class inequities, and patriarchal entitlement that have so scarred the American landscape and so crippled American democracy.

2

In the flood waters of Hurricane Katrina everything about the social, economic, and racial injustice of American society floated to the surface. Nothing could be hidden from news cameras on the scene; no sanitized "spin" could be given to the unfolding catastrophe. Hurricanes, of course, are a force of Nature; they do not discriminate. However, government and legislative actions, judicial decisions, and environmental policies inflict and sustain a myriad of social injustices that do discriminate, and the inequities of such long-standing injustices could not be denied, assuaged, or otherwise mitigated as the flood waters rose. As a result the poor in Louisiana, Mississippi and Alabama (and later in Texas with Hurricane Rita) suffered the most. The overwhelming majority of the poor in those states are African-American, Latino/a, Native American, the aged and the disabled. These are precisely the people we saw abandoned for days without food or water in the chaos created by city, state, and Federal officials.

The French Quarter in New Orleans, which experienced little flooding, and is the main tourist section of the city, is also virtually all-white. The nearby Ninth Ward, which suffered very extensive flooding because it is well below sea level, is almost 100% African-American, and 75% of its residents were living below *half* the poverty level. Mississippi and Louisiana are tied for the highest infant mortality rate in the United States (10.3 per 1,000 births), and Louisiana has the largest percentage of children living in poverty of any state, at 30%.

According to the Army Corps of Engineers, the levees in New Orleans had not been properly repaired or maintained since 1985 because of budget cuts at both the Federal and state levels, and by October 7, 2005 "the first independent experts to examine the New Orleans levees said that the walls on two critical canals gave way as the pressure from the flood waters ripped through the soil beneath them, shoving one of the earthen bases as far as 35 feet into a nearby neighborhood." Likewise, governmental and environmental policies over the past hundred years allowing for the continuing erosion and destruction of the wetlands in Louisiana and Mississippi contributed to the causes and effects of the devastation, according to scientific articles proliferating in newspapers and journals.

Similarly, Dr. Paul R. Epstein, writing in *The New England Journal of Medicine* (vol. 353, no. 14) in October 2005, analyzed the catastrophic effects of global warming citing extreme and unpredictable weather conditions all over the globe, and specifically citing the greater strength of hurricanes and tropical storms originating in the Atlantic as they hit the warm waters of the Gulf of Mexico. Dr. Epstein, an expert in public health, warned of the effects on all life forms. The melting of polar ice is accelerating at an alarming rate. He noted that "humans are playing a major role in causing these changes, largely through deforestation and the combustion of fossil fuels that produce heat-trapping gases such as carbon dioxide."

These reports and findings seem particularly critical in the wake of Hurricanes Katrina, Rita and Stan (along the Central American coast in October 2005) and the continuing refusal of the Bush administration to acknowledge the human responsibility for environmental degradation and global warming, its withdrawal from the Kyoto Accords on Global Warming, and its continuing reliance upon and expansion of fossil fuels and oil production.

3

While the focus of the media in the aftermath of Hurricane Katrina was on New Orleans, Mississippi and portions of Alabama were also devastated. A friend of mine traveling in Mississippi wrote us a collective email reporting that he was completely unprepared for the devastation he saw in Gulfport and Biloxi, everything literally flattened.

In addition to the devastation sustained by African-American communities, other peoples of color, also disenfranchised and marginalized, were equally battered. It is estimated that 120,000 Latinos, most of them Honduran, survivors of Hurricane Mitch in 1995, were living in Louisiana. They have been receiving only limited relief. Some are undocumented, and despite assurances from the Honduran Ambassador to the United States that there would be a moratorium on deportations (he said he had this in writing from the INS) most Hondurans would not go to the Red Cross facilities or apply for relief from FEMA because they were so fearful of *La Migra.* In any case, FEMA limits its resources to US citizens and permanent residents only. Likewise, the Council of Indian Nations and the American Indian Relief Agency have reported that there are five tribes in the Louisiana-Mississippi region that were devastated by the hurricane and that they are receiving very limited state and Federal assistance. These tribes are the Tunica-Biloxi, the Caddo, the Houmas, the Attakapas, and the Opelousas.

Prisoners in the New Orleans jail were left in their cells until flood waters were chest high, and then moved to a temporary jail at the Greyhound bus station. Law enforcement continued arrests in the midst of rescue operations, designating African Americans as looters, while whites, also loading up on water, food, and diapers were legitimately "seeking necessities" and either ignored or actually *assisted!* This was according to an eyewitness report by two paramedics from San Francisco, Larry Bradshaw and Lorrie Beth Slonsky, trapped in New Orleans while attending a convention.

Moreover, fantastic rumors were circulated and reported on the national media as fact (about rapes and murders of children in the Superdome), which proved to be completely unfounded, a fact acknowledged eventually even by the sheriff's department. Meanwhile, African-American and white survivors trying to walk across the New Orleans Bridge on the Pontchartrain Expressway were turned back by sheriffs who fired their weapons over their heads. The survivors had been told that buses were waiting across the bridge to take them out of the area. This turned out to be untrue, while the heavily armed sheriffs at the bridge were turning people back to protect property in the suburb of Gretna. Again, this is from eyewitness reports.

The same structures of racial and class injustice in place before the Hurricane were enacted and reinforced even as the rescue operations proceeded. With five days warning, a mandatory evacuation of the city of New Orleans was ordered. People with money, with cars, and with resources got out. Those hundreds of thousands in poverty, without cars, and/or without money for gas were left to fend for themselves. When public outrage and political fallout followed, Federal, state, and local officials, and police agencies, blamed the victims for the ensuing "chaos and anarchy." Indifferent to the plight of the poor, the aged, and the infirm, these same officials finally rallied; one could not help but feel it was primarily to save their own political careers.

And yet in spite of all of this, ordinary people, Black and white, Latino and Native American, men and women and children, in boats, on foot, on rooftops and in makeshift shelters, helped each other, and did the best they could to rescue each other and provide whatever relief might be possible. Apparently even some gang members in the convention center, so feared by the police, were actually one of the few organized groups who, according to witnesses, foraged for water and food, supplying the elderly and the very young first.

4

And now in the aftermath? Who will rebuild New Orleans? Gulfport? Biloxi? Who will make the decisions about bull-dozing whole sections of the city, including hospitals that have traditionally provided services to the poor? Who will make decisions about saving or destroying the largely working-class/African-American Southern University at New Orleans and the historically Black Xavier College? What corporations and contractors will get the money Congress has allocated to rebuild? Who will get the jobs? Who will be allowed and encouraged to return to Louisiana and Mississippi? Now, in mid-October 2005, there is a big land grab in progress as the rich and powerful return, reorganize, and get ready to re-establish themselves, and change New Orleans's political districting, with an eye towards future elections.

However, with the eyes of the public and the eyes of the world more clearly in focus, there is before us, all of us, a great opportunity to undo the decades of indignities and brutal poverty. There is a great opportunity to re-vision Louisiana and Mississippi, to *envision* a new Reconstruction, kindling the promise of the 1870s into a new political alignment, with grassroots coalitions to revitalize the wetlands, safely reconstruct and maintain the levees, build schools, housing, hospitals, child-care and cultural centers, parks, and libraries, provide jobs, and above all hope.

The actress Beah Richards, in one of her last interviews before her death in 2000, said that "The opposite of love is not hate; the opposite of love is *indifference*." This is, of course, precisely the politics of indifference we saw in Louisiana and Mississippi. Actor Danny Glover, participating in a gala concert to raise money for the reconstruction, observed that, "Hurricane Katrina revealed, more than anything else, a poverty of *imagination*."

May we have the courage and resourcefulness of six-year-old Deamonte Love, to walk down a new road, holding hands.

11

Cancer Alley
and Anti-Immigrant Reaction
in the Eye of the Storm

José T. Bravo
and Arnoldo García

Before Katrina hit there was already a great impact from contamination along the eighty-mile corridor from New Orleans to Baton Rouge, Louisiana. Communities consisting of mostly poor African-American residents along this eighty-mile stretch have come to call this area Cancer Alley. These residents have been living next to highly polluting industries for many years. Many residents have been very active in exposing these issues at all levels of government; they have crammed meeting halls with children and elders who have been affected by the contamination.

Cancer Alley is the epitome of "Environmental Racism"— where white communities have received more protection, compensation and remediation from contamination, while communities of color continue to be cited with pollution.

The media approach to Katrina has thrown the spotlight on New Orleans, obscuring and suppressing the environmentally racist impacts of the hurricane. This is part of a general historical lack of information about the communities along Cancer Alley. The "toxic gumbo" being touted in the media that emerged in the wake of the hurricane's sweep was already devastating communities of color and working people long before Katrina hit. Katrina exposed the deadly intersection of race, poverty, immigration status and toxic waste, but dangerous environmental conditions already existed.

Even when media coverage brings up environmental issues related to agriculture and the fishing industry along the Gulf Coast, and how it will suffer for many years, immigrants of color, mainly Latinos and Asians who work in these industries, are left out of the picture. Meanwhile, industries are encouraged by the government to get back on line as soon as possible, in order to minimize the impact on consumers who are hundreds and even thousands of miles away.

In plain language, this means that all the past wrongs could be and are probably going to be forgiven. The region is on the cusp of a free-for-all attack on regulations, monitoring and enforcement, which puts workers and communities in even greater danger.

The first symptom of this deregulation fever was set in motion when President Bush deferred two laws and undermined protections for working-class people in one fell swoop. Bush, claiming sympathy for those who lost documents, suspended the I-9 or employer sanctions law, which requires all new hires to prove "authorization" to work in the United States. Then, asserting that he wanted Federal aid to go further, Bush suspended the Davis-Bacon Act, which required that all employers pay the regional prevailing wage in Federal construction initiatives. Now Federal environmental regulations and protections are probably not far behind.

This two-pronged attack exposed immigrant and non-immigrant communities of color to unprecedented and ongoing threats to their return and the rebuilding of their homes. Contract workers, overwhelmingly immigrant, brought in from outside the region for cleanup and reconstruction, were subjected to dangerous exploitation, given inadequate water, shelter, and thoroughly inadequate equipment for hazardous work. Latinos, or anyone who "looked or sounded" foreign, were evicted *en masse* from Red Cross shelters, accused of being undocumented immigrants or contracted laborers who were not pre-hurricane residents, stopping them from seeking disaster relief. Immigrant contract workers were being abandoned by their employers in the bayou, in the streets or, if they were lucky, in Red Cross shelters, where they were harassed, evicted, and denied assistance.

Katrina made unwilling refugees of millions of people in the Gulf Coast region. For tens of thousands of Gulf residents, this was not the first time they were forced to flee their homes. Some 30,000 Vietnamese in Louisiana lost homes, jobs, and in some cases, their livelihood as fishermen. 40,000 Mexicans, mostly from New Orleans, were also forcibly displaced by the hurricane, as were other Central Americans in the region, including over 150,000 Hondurans and almost 10,000 Salvadorans, many of whom, like the Vietnamese, had already lost their homes to civil wars and hurricanes.

Immigrant communities faced additional danger as the storm subsided in August: individuals and organizations associated with the leading right-wing, anti-immigrant group, the Federation for American Immigration Reform, began a campaign calling on Congress to deny all FEMA relief to undocumented immigrants. This was the result of a different type of storm that was devastating immigrant communities across the country prior to Katrina: an anti-immigrant movement spurred by the Minutemen, armed vigilante and racist groups harassing immigrants, day laborers, and patrolling border and non-border communities supposedly looking for undocumented immigrants.

So the onslaught of attacks on environmental and economic justice is in full force down in the Big Easy. African Americans, immigrants, and working people are bearing the brunt of the political disaster that is rising from the ruins of Katrina.

12

Let the People Run It!

Curtis Reliford

This interview with Curtis Reliford was conducted by John Brown Childs in Santa Cruz, California, October 14, 2005, where Mr. Reliford was organizing the collection of relief supplies to take on his second truck trip to Louisiana. Born and raised in the African-American community of Shreveport, Louisiana, he now lives in Santa Cruz, where he is a landscaper and owner of Country Gentleman's Landscaping. Mr. Reliford is active in community organizations, including the NAACP and Brothers Helping Brothers.

I'm from Louisiana. My name is Curtis Reliford; I'm from Shreveport, born and raised there. I've lived here in Santa Cruz for twenty-one years. I left the south because there was no work for me. I was angry and rejected and got into some bad behavior. So, I just said, you know what, I'm leaving here. So I came to Santa Cruz.

What brought all of this work that I'm doing organizing and gathering supplies is my sister told me what was going on. I don't usually watch television. But when I saw that storm at lunchtime at a store I said, "That's a pretty serious hurricane." So I called my sister in Louisiana and she said "Yeah, it's bad. And the bad thing about it is that the people up here ain't getting shit."—excuse my language. So I called my mom on the other side of town and she said, "They ain't getting nothing over here either. We don't know what's going on." Then I called my grandma on the other side of town and she said the same thing: "Nothing over here."

It was sad. But it didn't really hit me then. So I went back to my work, landscaping, pulling up weeds. And then it came over me. I started thinking about when I first left Louisiana, about the racism, and about how some people just don't give a darn. They talk to you like you got a tail. And all of that started coming up. It was anger. I was so angry. I just was sitting there with anger. So I said to myself, What can I do to help? What's positive that I can do? So I decided to go make a flier like I do for Martin Luther King Day every year, just put it out there for anyone who wanted to go in with me to help the people there. I made the flier and went over to a friend's house, to Pat's, to check the grammar and all of that.

He was going to a city meeting and they were talking about what Santa Cruz can do. We went. He told them what I was doing. I am saying to myself, This is a God-sent thing. I asked God, Why do you want me to do this, of all people? So I told this meeting of the city council and other people that I had a whole plan on what to do and how to do it from Santa Cruz. I ran it down to them. It was perfect. It fit in with what they wanted to do. So I ran with it. Believe me the timing of all this is the reason I believe so strongly that it was a God thing. People, when they saw what I was doing, were all asking for a volunteer job, saying "What can I do, what can I do?" I had something for everyone to do. I had over a hundred people there. I checked with people in Louisiana about what they needed. We put all the supplies together, then ten of us went down there, driving our trucks, in eight days.

When we got there it wasn't what I expected. We had to regroup and reorganize. When we got there, the people in charge wanted me to take it to warehouses and drop all the supplies there. But I said, "I didn't come three thousand miles just to put all this in some kind of warehouse. I came to give it to the people, eye to eye. I'm not dropping this off here."

They said, "Well, you're going to have a hard time, you're going to run into this and that." But I told them, "OK, I'll run into it." So we went back into the city. We went to the Superdome to try to get in there. The National Guard were there and the police. I just drove up, the convoy with the US flags all over the trucks, and our signs saying "From Santa Cruz to New Orleans." They didn't want to let me in. So I really got up in their face and just said, "Man, we came three thousand miles to bring this stuff to people. The whole city of Santa Cruz is in an uproar trying to help. It took us three weeks to put this stuff together. So now you're saying we can't do this? We don't accept that."

So this National Guardsman called the police over, because I was talking some angry talk. The police came and I told him the same thing. "We came all the way across country to give this stuff to people. Can't you understand that?" I had tears in my eyes. I said, "You know what, you're just going to have to take me to jail, because I'm not leaving. It just ain't right."

So then he called the head of the Red Cross and I talked to him. I guess he felt me, what I was saying. Then a man who runs the Superdome came up and I told him the same thing. So, they're looking at all this stuff that we have and finally they said, "Come back tomorrow." But of course we had no place to go to park but they began to cooperate and said we could put the trucks right there.

The next day we had to work out something about how to get in, how to get up in the front to give out the stuff. The preachers down there saw us and they asked, "How did you get up in there? You're the only Black person we've seen allowed in there doing this." Because you see it was all these big corporations and organizations there in the front. And there I am, the only Black person allowed in to help, so what's wrong with that picture?

Then we sat there and just talked to people. There was this little old Black lady, one hundred and five years old in a wheelchair, and her sister, eighty-five years old, we were talking to. She said that she sat in her house for three days, and the water rose all the way up to her neck before anyone came and got her. Her sister got separated and she went from New Orleans to Lake Charles, from Lake Charles to Galveston, Texas to Houston, and then all the way back to Louisiana. And that story gave me strength, because if that one-hundred-and-five-year-old lady could do that, then I know I can do my best and not give up right now.

I think that the hurricane is a wakeup call for all us people to come together. And you know what? Black people need to get together. We need to do a better job of that. But the only thing I fault the government for is their consciousness. They need to help people to help themselves. But their consciousness is all about money, ruling, and running things. We're just people. They don't care about people. Their education has got in the way, and their status, and all of that. They're more concerned about that then they are about the people themselves.

And if you need some ideas about how to rebuild, call me; I'll tell you. That's what I do. I know how to clean it up. Give me a thousand workers; I'll go down and clean it up in five years.

If I could do anything, I would say they didn't come to your rescue in the first place. Shut it down, let the people run it. Start it all over, see what the people come up with.

13

New Orleans and the Gulf Coast Require an "Ethical Reconstruction Commission"

Rev. Nelson Johnson / Interfaith Workers Justice[1]

The fury of Hurricane Katrina combined with the accumulated effects of years of racism, poverty, and flawed assumptions have wrought a tragedy of Biblical and constitutional proportions.[2] The suffering, death, and destruction in New Orleans and the Gulf Coast region provide an opportunity not only for the outpouring of compassion around rescue and temporary shelter, but for an assessment of our priorities and way of life that have contributed to and magnified this tragedy.

We have been summoned by tragic circumstances to gather at this place. The pictures of thousands of desperate

---

[1] This essay originally appeared as a press release of the Interfaith Workers Justice coalition. It is reproduced here by permission of Rev. Johnson.

[2] The United States Constitution was established in order to form a more perfect union, establish justice, insure domestic tranquility, provide for the common defense, promote the general welfare, and secure the blessings of liberty to ourselves and posterity. See the *Preamble to the US Constitution* [footnote in original press release].

poor people trapped in a death bowl of rising toxic water summon us here. The agonizing cries of hungry children clinging to their mothers summon us here. Thousands of people living in squalor and fear in the Superdome summon us here. The knowledge that our elderly were left in hospitals and nursing homes to drown summon us here. The fact that 87% of New Orleans was inhabited by the descendants of slaves who were denied ethical reconstruction a hundred and forty years ago summons us here.

Natural, social, economic, political, and spiritual factors converged to cause tens of thousands of destroyed lives and an uninhabitable city in a devastated region. This was not mainly the might of the Hurricane, but the sins of us humans. We must now take responsibility for charting a new direction. Reconstruction will not only require large sums of money, it will also require facing old questions we have long denied about racism and poverty, and new questions we have tried to ignore: questions about our relationship to the earth and the toll of our ways of living on its capacity to renew itself. It is in this spirit that Interfaith Workers Justice together with religious and labor allies call for an "Ethical Reconstruction Commission" to assess, oversee, and guide a process of ethical reconstruction of New Orleans and the Region.

Over the last several weeks, we have witnessed a tremendous outpouring of compassion and caring, demonstrating once again the human capacity for love and generosity. That compassion and love must now be turned toward the challenging task of the ethical reconstruction of New Orleans and the region and the lives of hundreds of thousands of people. There are many different ways to approach this awesome task. Some want to move quickly with a top-down politicized process. We believe such an approach will not work. We believe that a process guided by the deepest ethics in our culture, and involving the broadest range of people affected, holds the only promise for the ethical reconstruction of the region and its inhabitants, and has the potential for setting a new direction for the nation.

The fate of New Orleans and the Gulf Coast, although tragic, provides a historical opportunity to learn painful lessons from our past, lessons that should be immediately put into play. Racism and poverty should be forever removed from being the underlying sources of such horrific suffering and death. We are challenged to build measures of restorative justice into every aspect of the reconstruction process; to rethink the basis of our relationships to each other and to the earth itself. Comprehensive worker justice in particular should become a theme for the entire rebuilding initiative. Worker injustice is not a natural disaster. It is a human sin.

Interfaith Worker Justice and many religious and labor partners call on Congress to establish an "Ethical Reconstruction Commission" in collaboration with religious and other civic leaders. The tragedy of New Orleans and the Gulf Coast cannot be allowed to descend into disguised, sophisticated quick moneymaking schemes by those with power and privilege at the expense of those who have already suffered too much. A compassionate and competent Ethical Reconstruction Commission is needed to guide the nation in facing the task of rebuilding lives and communities. It is needed to oversee the use of reconstruction funds, provide a voice for the people of the region, ensure that worker justice is central to the rebuilding, and offer overall guidance and ethical leadership to this initiative. We believe that the religious community should play a major role in the formation of such a Commission.

We further propose that among the first acts of this Commission would be to ensure the reinstatement of a living wage for all those whose skill, strength, and imagination will be called upon to rebuild the life of New Orleans, the region, and its people. Also immediate measures should be taken to ensure that the basic human rights of the people of this area are protected. These rights include the right to safe working conditions, protection of worker justice, environmental, health, and safety standards, and a concern for the well-being of neighborhoods and communities. They include the protection of the political rights of those who have not only been displaced but disenfranchised by this tragedy.

We encourage the following particular actions:

1. The restoration of the Davis-Bacon Act, which ensures paying the prevailing wage for work in the region.[3]

2. The provision of basic family support to all people in the region, regardless of immigration status. This package should include:

   Extended unemployment insurance and disaster unemployment insurance

   Comprehensive re-employment services

   Expansion of core food and health care services, such as food stamps, WIC [Women/Infants/Children], and Medicaid.[4]

3. The engagement of young people in the reconstruction process through massive job training programs, providing them with skills to not only rebuild their communities but also to rebuild their lives and put them on a productive job track for life.

In conclusion, the citizen-based Ethical Reconstruction Commission will ensure that the victims of this storm are provided not only the most basic necessities of life but are restored to full and productive lives in communities they have helped revision and rebuild. The Commission will also

---

[3]Editor's note: President Bush suspended the Davis-Bacon Act right after Katrina.
[4]Editor's note: As this book went to press, Governor of Florida Jeb Bush, brother of the President, had just cut Medicaid benefits in that state, with the approval of the Federal Government. This is being touted as a "model" for the nation.

oversee all contracts ensuring that public dollars serve the public benefit that jobs created serve the region's displaced workers, and that the priorities for rebuilding reflect the priorities of the people whose life and work gave the region its former vitality. Currently the poor who were left behind in the evacuation are being left behind in the planning for reconstruction. Except for the immediate New Orleans cleanup and repairs of water and utility systems, the signing of contracts and rebuilding of the region should stop until systems are in place for the broader public oversight.

Katrina was both a natural tragedy and a human tragedy. The reconstruction of New Orleans and the region offers opportunities not only to rebuild but also to rethink our priorities. "No longer will they build houses and others live in them, or plant and others eat, for as the days of a tree, so will be the days of my people. The people will enjoy the works of their hands" (Isaiah 65:22).

In the late 1960s Dr. Martin Luther King, facing the crisis of our cities, called for a revolution of values. In his prophetic and powerful words we affirm that, "Now is the time for America to rise up and live out the true meaning of her creed . . . that all men are created equal and endowed by their creator with certain inalienable rights among which are life, liberty, and the pursuit of happiness." The winds of Katrina have cleared the way for all of us to work toward the fulfillment of this promise.

14

We Have Lost Our Citizenship Again

Katrina's aftermath: The new Dred Scott

Rebecca Hall

African Americans: We have lost our citizenship again.

Just before the Civil war, a reactionary Supreme Court, not unlike the one that Bush II is now constructing, decided that the escaped slave named Dred Scott could be returned to enslavement despite the fact that he had lived for more than ten years in Minnesota where slavery had been made illegal. Overturning statute and precedent, the Court held that Blacks, free or slave, were not citizens of this nation. The Court ruled that they had no rights which the white man was bound to respect; and that the "negro" might justly and lawfully be reduced to slavery for his benefit. . . .

Despite our presence in this country since at least 1619; despite the fact that we were instrumental in building this country, including the very buildings in which the three branches of government are housed; despite our stolen labor; our citizenship was denied then and it is being denied now.

What is a citizen? According to *Black's Law Dictionary*, a citizen is a person who under the Constitution "is a member of the political community, owing allegiance and being entitled to the enjoyment of full civil rights." Citizens are full members of a community, who have "established or submitted themselves to the dominion of a government for the promotion of their general welfare and the protection of their individual and collective rights" (Fifth abridged edition, 1993).

What are we to think of "general welfare" and "protection" when my people lay dying by the hundreds, while the Navy's multipurpose amphibious assault and rescue ship, the USS Bataan, sat in the Gulf of Mexico with all of its formidable medical facilities? The USS Bataan was not brought in until four days after the hurricane, which is after the "golden seventy-two hours" in which rescuing people alive rather than recovering dead bodies is so essential (Navy/Military news Web site).

African Americans were rounded up and tightly packed into the Superdome, as in some monster slave ship of the infamous "middle passage" on the ocean of flood waters. They were held like captives in the slave-pen barracoons, without food and water, awaiting the slow-to-arrive school buses that would, like slave ships, disperse them throughout a land far away from their homes. As just as slavery's apologists proclaimed the benefits of that destructive institution, Barbara Bush, surveying the humanitarian disaster of displaced people in the Houston Astrodome, assured us that "since so many of the people are underprivileged, this is working very well for them." And, to add insult to injury, "shelters" scattered along the Interstate 10 highway were locked down at night like prisons.

So, are we citizens?

The government's lack of response and the nature of what response it did make shows me that we are not.

After the Civil War, the Fourteenth Amendment to the US Constitution explicitly overruled the Dred Scott case by stating that all those born in the United States are citizens, and that they are entitled to all the privileges and protections thereof. When I go through my day, images invade my thoughts—old people dying in nursing homes; the young and the sick slowly drowning in their attics; the thousands with nothing, not even water to drink, in temperatures above 100° for four days, and I am terrified. I think—where is the support structure that we have been taught to believe in? Where are the resources of what we are constantly told is the richest and most powerful country on earth? This country got needed aid to tsunami victims on the other side of the world in twenty-four hours.

How can I know that if my mother was in a nursing home in a disaster, our government would lift a finger to help her? What if it were my child who needed medical care? How can I be sure of anything anymore?

Ain't I a citizen?

I think not.

Why do I make the analogy with Dred Scott? I do so because this is much more than a huge mistake made by the government that happened to fail African Americans on this occasion. It is in fact symptomatic of a broader abrogation of citizenship that has been underway for years, and which has finally been effected by Bush the Second. We already know not to expect an ambulance to come anytime soon if we call 911 from a Black neighborhood. We already know to expect trouble if caught driving while Black.

Sometimes I forget to remember these facts. But this latest Dred Scott shows us that our lack of citizenship is finally complete and we are refugees in a foreign land.

References

Black's Law Dictionary, fifth abridged edition, West Publishing Company, St. Paul, Minnesota (1983).

Navy/Military News: www.news.navy.mil/search/displayasp?story_id+19694

15

Katrina Poses the Question:
What Are the Duties of Governments
to Their People?

Jeremy Brecher

If George Bush had sent an army to Louisiana, leveled the city of New Orleans, killed a thousand or more residents, and driven hundreds of thousands from their homes, it would be regarded as a crime against humanity under international law. What is it when the same result is accomplished not by malfeasance but by nonfeasance?

Katrina should provoke a great debate on the role of government in American society. One theme in that debate should be the fundamental duties of governments to their people under international human rights principles.

While the purpose of the US Constitution as stated in the Preamble includes "to promote the general welfare," the rights actually spelled out in it often take a negative form: "Congress shall make no law . . ." But modern international human rights perspectives provide much more affirmative obligations on the part of governments.

International law, for example, provides clear require-ments concerning "internal displacement" of people—codified in the *UN Guiding Principles on Internal Displacement*. Any investigation of the Federal response to Katrina should examine whether the US government and the Bush administration have systematically violated rights like these:

* Internally displaced persons have the right to request and receive protection and humanitarian assistance from national authorities.

* All internally displaced persons have the right to an adequate standard of living.

* All wounded and sick internally displaced persons as well as those with disabilities shall receive to the fullest extent possible and with the least possible delay, the medical care and attention they require, without distinction on any grounds other than medical ones.

* Competent authorities have the primary duty and responsibility to establish conditions, as well as provide the means, which allow internally displaced persons to return voluntarily, in safety and with dignity, to their homes or places of habitual residence, or to resettle voluntarily in another part of the country.

* Special efforts should be made to ensure the full participation of internally displaced persons in the planning and management of their return or resettlement and reintegration.

* The guiding principles shall be applied without discrim-ination of any kind, such as race, color, sex, language, religion or belief, political or other opinion, national, ethnic or social origin, legal or social status, age, disability, property, birth, or on any other similar criteria.

The human rights responsibilities of the United States government were neglected long before Katrina made landfall. At the very least, governments have a duty to protect the lives of their people. The US government did not send an army to kill people in New Orleans (at least not before Katrina struck), but those who died were surely the victims of the government's failure in its duty to protect their lives. Today they are just as dead as they would have been if the government had deliberately undermined the levees so that when a storm came they would break.

But Katrina revealed even more disturbing failures of the US government to protect the human rights of its people. The International Covenant on Economic, Social and Cultural Rights and the Universal Declaration of Human Rights establish the right to an adequate standard of living, including the right to food, health, water, necessary social services, and housing. As it laid bare New Orleans's concealed poverty and discrimination, Katrina revealed what the American government and media strive to hide: The United States systematically denies basic human economic rights to a substantial portion of its people. And those rights are denied disproportionately to African Americans, Latinos, immigrants, and other minorities—a discrimination which in itself is a violation of human rights.

There are no rights without duties, and international law places the duty to protect human rights first and foremost on governments. As one expert recently wrote,

> A State cannot pretend absolute sovereignty without demon-strating a duty to protect people's rights. . . . The sovereignty of States is no longer based on the right of Governments, kings, sheikhs or presidents to govern; it depends on their duty when governing to respect human beings.[1]

As the United States debates the future role of government, guaranteeing the internationally recognized human rights of its people should be declared its binding duty.

---

[1] Vesselin Popovski, "Sovereignty as Duty to Protect Human Rights," UN Chronicle Online Edition, www.un.org/Pubs/chronicle/2004/issue4/0404p16.html.

16

The Tragedy of Katrina:
Will There Be a Presidential Apology?

Rickie Sanders

"I will never apologize for the United States of America; I don't care what the facts are."
—George Herbert Walker Bush,
Newsweek, August 15, 1989,
after an Iranian airliner
was mistakenly shot down
by the US warship Vincennes,
killing 290 civilians)

Q: *Sir, you talk about fixing what's wrong and you talk about the results not being acceptable, but there are a lot of people wondering why you weren't fixing the problems yesterday or the day before, and why the richest country on Earth can't get food and water to those people that need it?*

The President: *The levees broke on Tuesday in New Orleans. On Wednesday, we– and Thursday we started evacuating people...*
> —George W. Bush, September 2, 2005,
> responding to a reporter's question

Suppose that tomorrow the President issued a national apology for the country's failure to protect the citizens of New Orleans from the ravages of hurricane Katrina. It would certainly not be inappropriate—acknowledging wrongdoing (failing to act responsibly in a timely manner or acting irresponsibly) almost always begins with a formal apology. The events surrounding Katrina point to wrongdoing, either because of bumbling incompetence on the part of those chosen to lead or the belief that race is a morally relevant difference and differential treatment of people of color can be justified.

Were the President to offer an apology, it would certainly not be the first time a country or leader would have issued a public apology. The Catholic Church recently issued a formal apology to victims of sex abuse at the hands of priests. It acknowledged that it failed to respond appropriately. In a recent *New York Times* article, Seth Stevenson lists several countries that have in the past made national apologies, e.g. Poland formally apologized for the mass killings of Jews in Polish concentration camps; Germany accepted responsibility—and issued a formal apology—for its role in the holocaust; Switzerland offered words of conciliation and established a reparations fund (but many Jews feel it has yet to make full amends for its role as banker to the Nazi party). Bill Clinton was widely criticized for *considering* a national apology for slavery, but was successful in securing a national apology to the victims of unethical radiation experiments conducted during the Cold War. He also offered the nation's apology to the survivors of the Tuskegee medical study that denied treatment to 399 African-American men.

Ronald Reagan apologized to Japanese Americans placed in internment camps and Congress awarded $20,000 to each internee. And according to a CBS news story in 1995, the United States was forced to apologize to Japan in 1995 when a twelve-year-old girl was raped by three US servicemen in Okinawa.

> I'm here to request in the most humble and sincere manner that you accept the apology of the people of the United States and the US Navy, as a personal representative of President Bush.
>
> —Admiral William J. Fallon,
> the Vice Chief of Naval Operations,
> Bush administration Special Envoy to Japan,
> apologizing to the Japanese
> for the sinking of a Japanese trawler
> that left nine people lost at sea
> (USA Today, 2/24/2001)

Bill Clinton offered a formal apology for the failure of the international community to respond in a timely manner when the details of mass killings and genocide in Rwanda became known. Can we expect a similar response from George Bush to the events in New Orleans? The President and Congress held a midnight session about the health care of Terri Schiavo—one woman. Why did this not happen in the first twenty-four hours of Katrina in reaction to the news of hundreds dying unspeakable deaths?

All this leads to questions: When is a national apology appropriate? What does it mean for the President to say, "I'm sorry. I accept responsibility."? What should it entail? Exactly what does a national apology mean? Should the victims of Katrina be given an apology for the serious lapse of twenty-four hours when their government failed to hear their cries? If not, why not? When are apologies sensible? What is the justice goal to be accomplished by *not* apologizing? What is the justice goal of apologizing? When does the larger goal of social justice override a nation's desire to appear "right?" When is an apology undeniably necessary to serve a larger good? What needs to happen to make an apology meaningful? Questions such as these are based on normative considerations of what should be or ought to be. It is because making value and moral judgments is so much a part of human life that excluding them from a discussion of Katrina is impossible—and unethical.

Jacob Weisberg would argue that an apology is warranted if there is an indisputable misdeed. But there can't be too many. If apologies are dispensed indiscriminately and without care, they can be empty and insincere.

> I'm a boxer, and from now on, I will let my boxing talk for me . . . I shouldn't have done that . . . I just forgot he was a human being. I was no longer playing under the rules. Any kind of functional thinking, any kind of rational thinking, that was totally out the window. It's pretty embarrassing . . . I just totally lost it.
>
> —Mike Tyson "apologizing" to the boxing commission for his behavior in a fight with Evander Holyfield (June 28, 1997)

> He's sorry . . . I love him. I forgive him. It's not so much that he has to apologize, I already forgave him.
>
> —Evander Holyfield accepting Tyson's "apology" (June 28, 1997)

It is not difficult to distinguish between an apology driven by a desire to uphold a moral code and one with no immediate moral content. If I step on your foot and offer an apology, it merely identifies me as an appropriately socialized individual. However, if a government does nothing as it observes its citizens helpless, in need, and dying from lack of care , it is morally culpable. A national apology responds to a moral injustice. An apology made under these circumstances is purposive—designed to create a space for national (or international) healing and reconciliation and to create conditions that will allow two parties to move away from a state of injustice. With an apology, a country acknowledges the harm it caused and expresses empathy and respect for those harmed. The country assumes an active stance and takes responsibility for the damage done, not just the material damage, but equally important, the psychological, emotional, psychic, and mental damage. The Canadian Christian Church is instructive here. Over the years it has issued apologies to Aboriginal communities. The apologies range from a general recognition of the complex and problematic relationship between First Nations People and the European settlers to apologies that respond to very specific allegations. How would a national apology to the victims of Katrina (which includes everybody) look? What would it acknowledge?

Would it acknowledge the years of disinvestment in the levee system of New Orleans? Or the deliberately orchestrated creative destruction associated with the process of globalization that has led to unemployment and poverty? Would it accept responsibility for the pockets in New Orleans where people live lives resembling those in a Third World country, right alongside others who have some of the highest standards of living in the world? Or would it acknowledge that far too many people live lives of poverty and inequality compounded by violence and insecurity; or that their emotions congeal around survival mechanisms—fight or flight accompanied by despair, resentment, apathy, futility, fury, and rage. Or what about the fact that approximately 30% of New Orleanians did not have access to a car and in 1999, roughly 20% of the population had incomes below the poverty line? In constructing an apology, would the United States acknowledge the health crisis of forty million uninsured in the country? Or would it apologize to future generations for cutting taxes in the middle of a war and refusing to raise taxes to pay for its butchered response to the devastation wrought by Katrina, thus ensuring that future generations would foot the bill? Would it accept responsibility for the increasing rates of homelessness and poverty that plague not just New Orleans but the nation as a whole? What about the emergency evacuation apparatus? Would the apology include words to acknowledge that there was no emergency evacuation plan? It simply did not exist; it was all a sham.

Maybe that casts the net too far. Maybe the apology should be limited to the government's response during the twenty-four hours preceding and following the actual hit of the hurricane. In that case, would the government acknowledge its role in fostering feelings of betrayal; or the broken social contract that now exists between the government and its citizens? Would an apology address the humiliation experienced by those locked in the Superdome and the Convention Center (and the shame of those who survived and still, as of this writing, have to stand in line for hours just to get diapers for their children)? Would the government accept responsibility for the disrespectful treatment of the dead bodies floating amid raw sewerage in the floodwaters that breached untended levees? And what about the forced displacement, separation of families, and the failure of public officials to remember those whom they are charged to protect? A formal apology is needed. Acknowledging wrongdoing is the first step in beginning the healing and reconciliation process. But given all that has happened, acknowledging wrongdoing will require more than the simple act of saying "I'm sorry." An apology is not enough, but the road to justice begins there.

17

Katrina:
Giving Eyesight to the Blind

David Wellman

The last thing a fish sees is the water. Things that are not problematic seem natural; they tend to be inconspicuous, they are literally not seen. Fish take the water they swim in for granted in the same way white Americans take their race as normal, as a given. The taken-for-granted world of white Americans has, until recently, been their normality, not their whiteness. As a consequence, the privileges associated with being white have not been experienced as advantages. Instead, whiteness was experienced as just being "normal."

Hurricane Katrina did much more than crumble levees, put houses where highways used to be and turn streets into canals. She also rearranged the sociological landscape along the Gulf Coast. Katrina made the normal problematic, the inconspicuous conspicuous, and the invisible visible. Suddenly, white Americans could now see some of the water. In the space New Orleans used to be, they saw two cities where they thought there was one: a Black city and a white one, separate and unequal. They could see that whites were the minority and they had been quickly evacuated and relocated. They also saw an African-American majority that was trapped in the floods of wreckage and havoc.[1] For a brief moment, whiteness was not normal; it visibly represented advantage. Bessie Smith got it right in "Backwater Blues": "When it thunders and lightnin' and the wind begins to blow / There's thousands of people ain't got no place to go."

Like an earthquake, the fault lines Katrina exposed were neither random nor coincidental. They revealed patterns. Protected by the levees and set on higher ground, the largely white neighborhoods sustained the least amount of damage. Their wealthy inhabitants were able to drive themselves to higher ground and safety. One man even helicoptered in an Israeli security company to guard his Audubon Place house and those of his neighbors.[2] In sharp contrast, closer to the river in the lowlands, the nearly all-Black surrounding neighborhoods and parishes were devastated. Their inhabitants were locked out of any chance for escape and locked into the Superdome. Without cars or money and no buses to rescue them, they were left to fend for themselves or die. Although the mortality rates are not presently known, no one doubts they will reveal dramatic demographic patterns. Who got out and who got left had to do with the color of one's skin. Communities of color that were vulnerable before the hurricane were vulnerable in its wake. As with all "natural" disasters, Katrina made public the consequences of historically accumulated and deeply embedded racial inequality. She laid to rest the self-styled New Orleans mythical view of itself as racial "gumbo," the post modernist model of "hybridity."

Katrina didn't produce the racial fissures so vividly reflected on American television screens. She brought them to light; she reproduced them. She made Americans see them. But they didn't always see the same thing. Depending

---

[1]Blacks were 67.3% of New Orleans's population; whites were 28.1% (Figures compiled by the Urban Institute, using data from the 2000 US census).
[2]Christopher Cooper, "Old-line families plot the future," *The Wall Street Journal,* September 8, 2005.

on who the actors were, the same image evoked two distinctly different meanings. For example, one newspaper photo showing a white couple up to their chests in water, the woman holding bags of food, was captioned "finding bread and soda from a local grocery store." Another photo featured a young Black man also wading through chest-high water. He is holding a case of soda and pulling a floating bag. The caption read "looting a grocery store."[3]

This deep cognitive fault line could be heard as well as seen in the ways Americans talked about Katrina. Just as one image evoked two competing interpretations, whites and Blacks spoke of Katrina in very distinct terms. Whites focused on lawlessness. Blacks talked about desperation, exclusion, isolation and neglect. Blacks and whites drew dramatically different conclusions from the same hurricane. While African Americans spoke bitterly about being warehoused in the Astrodome, the President's mother saw things from another perspective. "So many of the people in the arena here were underprivileged anyway," Barbara Bush said after touring relocation facilities in Houston, "so this is working very well for them."[4] The findings of a national survey by the Pew Research Center for the People and the Press highlight the perceptual chasm that divides Black and white America. The survey discovered that 71% of Blacks say the disaster shows that racial inequality remains a major problem in the country. A majority of whites (56%), however, feel this was not a particularly important lesson of the disaster. Moreover, while 66% of Blacks think that the government's response to the crisis would have been faster if most of the storm's victims had been white, an even larger percentage of whites (77%) disagree.[5]

---

[3]Tania Ralli, "Who's a Looter? In Storm's Aftermath, Pictures Kick Up a Different Kind of Tempest," *The New York Times*, September 5, 2005.
[4]Quoted by Elisabeth Bumiller and Anne E. Kornblut, "Black Leaders Say Storm Forced Bush to Confront Issues of Race and Poverty," *The New York Times*, September 18, 2005.

Katrina also revealed that America has hardly become the "color-blind" society neo-conservative ideologues celebrate. Instead, the Category IV storm reminded Americans that old racist narratives die hard, living on, inaccessible to facts on the ground. Demonizing the stranded, the press reported complete degradation and violence running rampant in the Superdome. A week after Katrina hit, the Baton Rouge media reported that evacuees from New Orleans were carjacking, guns and knives were being seized in local shelters, riots were erupting. The local mayor responded predictably: "We do not want to inherit the looting and all the other foolishness that went on in New Orleans," Kip Holden told the *Baton Rouge Advocate*. "We do not want to inherit that breed that seeks to prey on other people." The trouble, wrote Howard Witt of the *Chicago Tribune*, is that "scarcely any of it was true—the police confiscated a single knife from a refugee in one Baton Rouge shelter. There were no riots in Baton Rouge. There were no armed hordes."[6]

Because Black and white Americans inhabit such different social locations and therefore had divergent experiences of Katrina, they had difficulty talking about why it took so long for the Federal government to rescue survivors of the storm. Blacks were less interested in why than when. White Americans, on the other hand, played the "blame game." For them, the issue was who could be held responsible for the failure to respond in a decisive and expeditious fashion. Who was the evildoer accountable for the negligence? After firing the most obvious individual—FEMA Director Michael Brown—President Bush thought he knew who was *not* responsible. "The storm didn't discriminate," he reportedly explained, "and neither did the rescuers."[7]

[5]The Pew Research Center for the People and the Press, "Two-in-Three Critical of Bush's Relief Efforts: Huge Racial Divide Over Katrina and Its Consequences," September 8, 2005.

[6]Gary Younge, "Murder and Rape—Fact or Fiction?" *The Guardian*, September 6, 2005.

[7]Quoted in *the New York Times*, September 13, 2005.

By transforming the normal into the problematic, Katrina makes it possible to see that this explanation is inadequate. Neither the storm nor the rescuers needed to discriminate to create the devastation that followed this hurricane. Because of historically accumulated and deeply embedded racial inequality, the poor and Black survivors needed rescuing *before* the storm slammed into New Orleans. Katrina exposed that carefully guarded secret.

Because the secret is out and our taken-for-granted world disrupted, the water we experience as normal has become problematic. Can we change its direction? Or do we simply wait "till human voices wake us, and we drown."[8]

---

[8]T. S. Eliot, "The Love Song of J. Alfred Prufrock".

18

Katrina:
Where the Natural and the Social Meet

Herman Gray

What makes Katrina and other natural disasters like it a social issue, and not simply an expression of the force of nature? And what specifically is social (as opposed to natural) about it—in this case, to what does the term social refer: The response and level of preparation of local, state, and national governments? The great outpourings of support, money, grief, shock, anger, outrage? Media coverage—especially with those spectacular television pictures and print photos of stranded citizens, flood waters, misery and desperation of the living with dead bodies in their midst, news reporters steeled against hurricane force winds? Perhaps the idea of the social refers to the reports of panic and mayhem at the Superdome (the very name is enough to conjure capabilities of extraordinary dimensions) and the New Orleans convention center, or it could just as easily refer to panic- and frustration-fueled urban legends of rampant looting, rape, and pillage among the mostly Black and poor *citizens* stranded in the face of a paralyzed and ineffective government and related relief agencies.

On the other hand, it is much easier to think of Katrina as a natural disaster—the hurricane-force winds, water and flooding, breaks in dikes and levees, lakes and rivers overrunning their banks and shores, toxins and pollutants released into the air and water. Day after day, in the immediate aftermath of the hurricane, the news media presented accounts of damage to property, loss of life, and threats to health and safety. There were also historical benchmarks against which to compare one disaster against the next—the firestorms in the Oakland, California hills; the Galveston hurricane of 1927; more recently, Hurricanes Camille and Andrew, the Indonesian tsunami, and killer earthquakes in Japan, Mexico, Turkey, and Iran. OK, fair enough. These inventories and narratives of nature's wrath are important and they make sense to us intuitively. Television pictures, historical comparisons, statistics of death and destruction all provide a means of helping us to locate ourselves, loved ones, friends and neighbors on the cultural and social map in catastrophes of such large scale. These data and the cumulative tolls they detail make sense to most of us as natural disasters—that is, events caused by the forces of nature; as such they often encourage a sense of inevitability and ultimately, resignation that clouds our willingness to understand these events socially, culturally and politically.

I want to suggest that there is an important social dimension to our very capacity to think, or not think, about this disaster and its related effects in all of its implications and ramifications. In other words, our national experience of Katrina is bound up with policy choices, resource commitments, notions of civic responsibility, and the role of government. Katrina is also shot through with the taken-for-granted, dare I say naturalized, frameworks by which we make sense of, imagine solutions, narrate stories, assign blame, and explain just how this very "natural" disaster wreaked so much social havoc and impacted so many lives. Here I want to deliberately trouble the boundary between the natural and the social. I want to disturb or unsettle the ease with which we assign things to the category of natural or social (making them more or less available for certain kinds of critical interrogations). In other words, the racial and class politics, the tensions between urban and suburban development, the enforcement of racial and class boundaries around geographical location, decisions (intentional or not) about just who was worthy of rescuing and who would be left behind—all of which produced so much of the moral and political outrage in the aftermath of the storm—were simply the surface expressions of social decisions, power relations, policy choices, and resource commitments which were in place long before Katrina appeared on the hurricane forecaster's map. These relations and the tensions they express constitute the terrain where the social and natural meet; what we intuitively understand as natural and the effects of forces purportedly beyond our control, on closer and more sustained critical reflection, show the operations of social relations and social logics. While experts in the media, and the public, refer to these phenomena as natural disasters, these matters are historically and socially produced and not just the inevitable results of weather, nature, or the will of a divine force.

By the time the national government's weak response to the disaster registered in the American public's imagination (largely through the media's stories and pictures), the social logics and social relations that determined the course of daily life in the neighborhoods, parishes, and towns along the banks of the Gulf of Mexico, Lake Pontchartrain, and the Mississippi River where Katrina landed was well established and fortified through decades of (in)action and studied benign neglect on the part of the Federal, state, and local agencies. Despite warnings (in the form of a *Times-Picayune* expose) about the vulnerability of New Orleans to a catastrophic hurricane, policy decisions (at the state and national level), resource commitments, and political machinations were deeply entrenched. What is more, the Bush administration (fueled by racial, class, and moral politics) aggressively pursued agendas aimed at shrinking the size and influence of the national government, while ensuring tax breaks for the wealthy, and relying on the private sector to achieve that which was once guaranteed by the state. These policy commitments exposed the most vulnerable segments of the society, those most in need of the resources of the state, to the combined destructive power of Hurricane Katrina and poverty. Meanwhile, in talk about rebuilding, the production of New Orleans as a tourist destination of endless fun, fantasy, and excitement—Mardi Gras, jazz, food, and drink—continues apace, a fantasy which of course depends on the isolation, containment, and displacement of the New Orleans that is 60+% Black and poor and concentrated in those geographical sectors of the city most vulnerable to natural and social catastrophe. Like Hartford, Detroit, Los Angeles, Oakland, and many of the nation's urban centers, this version of New Orleans has been abandoned by a national government whose commitment to the public good and collective responsibility for civil society has been replaced with religious fundamentalism, individual responsibility, corporate profits, and market principles.

In the face of powerful social, cultural, economic, and political forces it is easy to shift blame to desperate poor and Black citizens for making bad choices, for not getting out of flood areas, for deciding to ride out the storm, for looting, for simply being poor and Black. What is much harder to portray, even in dramatic pictures, is the routine (and deliberate) production of social policies that leave such populations to fend for themselves, to make the kind of choices—good, bad, or indifferent—that anyone in their situation might make. References to individuals, individual choices, character and moral judgments by those of us who would dare judge our neighbors and fellow citizens must at the very least be tempered by appreciating options which they face (or do not face), options that are socially produced and structured by public policy decisions. People make choices, sometimes wise, and at other times not so wise, within the context of their social and economic circumstance. We might call this the politics of survival. Value judgments about the wisdom of such choices, and the moral character of those who make them, appeal to vacuous notions of character and morality, and elide the fact that policies that produce such circumstances are social and not simply individual. In the wealthiest, most productive nation in the world, to make policy choices that reduce people to such survival tactics and then to blame them for a bad choice is the real disaster. These are not just matters of wind, rain, and floods, but also matters of public policy, political will, and a sense of the public good.

19

Language Matters:
Hurricane Katrina
and Media Responsibility

Wendy Cheng and
Michelle Denise Commander

The day after Hurricane Katrina hit the Gulf Coast, Yahoo! News posted hundreds of images, two of which sparked a flurry of intense discussions. While nearly identical in composition, the photographs had notably different captions. The first claimed to show a "young [Black] man" who had just "looted" a grocery store, while the second described two white "residents" who had just "found" bread and soda in a grocery store.

Regardless of whether the captions could have been explained by extenuating circumstances, when placed side by side, their racist implications became impossible for anyone to deny. Though the second image has since been removed by its source (AFP), we must seize the opportunity to have a much-needed conversation about media responsibility—before the damning images disappear not just from the Internet but from collective memory.

What is the ethical responsibility of the media when a natural disaster strikes? In the wake of Katrina, print and television media filled almost immediately with images of "disorder," "lawlessness" and "urban warfare."

Especially in post–Rodney King Los Angeles, we cannot escape the fact that these words evoke a class- and racially coded vision of urban "race riots." Defaulting to the language of this vision justified government negligence and seriously compromised the ability of the general public to empathize with all victims.

The abundance of depictions of New Orleans as a "menacing landscape of disorder and fear" (AP) overshadowed the conditions of poverty and segregation that trapped Katrina victims in a flooding city in the first place. Scenes of tragedy and loss became subsumed by fears personified by "lawless" individuals. Such media prioritization of the sensational formed the impression that if "civil order" had been maintained in the city, then the amount of devastation in New Orleans would not have been as great. Thus influenced, many Americans felt validated in pointing the finger of blame toward (a) minority (of) lawbreakers. Louisiana governor Kathleen Blanco's declaration of "war on looters" made headlines. Published and televised images of National Guard tanks rolling into the city foregrounded the guardsmen's "locked-and-loaded" M-16 rifles.[1]

Comparisons of the situation in New Orleans to Haiti and "other Third-World trouble spots" (Reuters) tapped into similarly problematic depictions of such places as chaotic sites of violent rebellion and so-called primitivism. Some media outlets also characterized Katrina survivors as "refugees," a term that commonly refers to persons forcibly displaced from a nation's borders. Granted, American exceptionalist connotations of the term "refugee" need their own corrective.

---

[1]Editor's note: We also now know that the private security firm Blackwater, known for its for-profit mercenary soldiers in Iraq, sent a contingent to New Orleans under the aegis of the Governor of Louisiana and the Department of Homeland Security.

Nevertheless, the implication that the rights and values of survivors were somehow alien to those of other Americans only exacerbated a general sense of disfranchisement among the racially and economically marginalized population.

Language choices are not just matters of political correctness (if, in fact, political correctness is ever "just" political correctness), nor are they arbitrary. They are drawn from specific histories of racial conflict and have real consequences. Certainly covering a disaster of such proportions involves tremendous difficulties and urgencies. Responsible reportage alone cannot correct a long succession of systemic inequalities. However, all members of the media must be cognizant of the potential racial and historical implications of their depictions. Refraining from employing and thereby perpetuating harmful stereotypes would be a start.

20

Katrina's Aftermath

Michael K. Brown

Disasters have a way of galvanizing Americans, and the response to Hurricane Katrina was overwhelming. They opened their pocketbooks—to date Americans have pledged or contributed more than a billion dollars to the American Red Cross—and volunteered their labor to rescue and assist those individuals displaced by the flooding and devastation in New Orleans and along the Gulf Coast. The generosity of ordinary American citizens starkly contrasts with the ineptitude of the government and its abandonment of the poor, mostly African Americans, who could not get out of the city. But Katrina exposed more than the cronyism and incompetence of a Republican administration used to getting its way. It ripped open the gauzy façade of a smug, complacent society and revealed the degradation and poverty that are consequences of deeply embedded racial inequality. Will the memory of who the victims were, and why they were in such desperate straits to survive, help us to renew a commitment to social justice, or will we forget?

The social geography revealed in the aftermath of Katrina is unmistakable. New Orleans is a highly segregated city where your location in relation to the color line depends on how far below sea level you are. The further a neighborhood is below sea level, the higher the number of African Americans and the higher the poverty rate. It is no accident that the floodwaters submerged Black neighborhoods while leaving the mostly white Garden district relatively dry.

Although the New Orleans port is the fifth largest in the world, linking the jugular vein of the American economy—the Mississippi river—to the rest of the world, the city's economy depends mostly on plenty of tourists flocking to the French Quarter to soak up the food, music and culture that sets New Orleans apart from all other American cities. Social class in New Orleans is not defined by any division between factory workers and owners but between the city's insular business establishment that runs the restaurants, hotels, and bars and a large (very) low wage platoon of cooks, waiters, dancers, janitors, housekeepers and others who man the city's service economy. Wages are low; the median wage for men and women is just 75% of the national median, about $30,000 a year, and almost a quarter of the city's residents are below the poverty line. Black income and wages lag substantially behind whites'; Black families in New Orleans take home just half of what white families do. The poverty rate in some Black neighborhoods is upwards of 40%.

It would be a mistake to think that somehow the racial inequality so apparent in New Orleans is all that different from other American cities. Take Atlanta, a city with a booming economy. Atlanta's poverty rate is higher than New Orleans's and the city is as deeply segregated. And the racial stratification in both cities is a product of the same forces: white flight fueled by racial hostility and government mortgage assistance, entrenched labor market discrimination, inadequate schools, and a lack of viable economic opportunities. All that sets New Orleans apart is its vulnerability to hurricanes, which has nothing to do with nature and everything to do with fifty years of rapacious building on wetlands and shortsighted flood-protection policies that failed to protect the city.

New Orleans will be rebuilt; the question is how and whether this disaster will revive an effort to finally confront the real legacy of our long history of racial oppression. At the moment things don't look so promising. Americans' generosity is time-limited, available only to the victims of disasters clearly beyond their control and even then only temporarily. Otherwise you are on your own. The aftermath of Hurricane Katrina did little to alter settled public views about poverty and race. According to a survey conducted by the Pew Research Center after the disaster, about two-fifths of Americans regard our leaky safety net as luxurious, believing that poor people have it easy because of government benefits. These views are, if anything, harsher than they were several years ago. Many people, about 60% of adults in the Pew surveys, believe that Blacks are poor because they don't try hard enough, not because of racial discrimination.

At the same time, the Republicans mouth compassionate platitudes, while they scheme to limit governmental assistance to the hurricane's victims, and to make the poor pay for rebuilding New Orleans. It is clear by now that George W. Bush and his minions have no intention of spending any more than they have to for relief, and they will prevent any changes in social policies that would make them, even temporarily, more generous. A case in point is Medicaid. This is about the only way that poor working people can get needed medical assistance, even in good times. President Bush opposes a Senate bill that would make Medicaid benefits available to all low-income Hurricane survivors paid for out of Federal revenues. Instead, the administration prefers to push the responsibility for providing medical aid to the affected state governments, but there are no guarantees the Federal government will pick up the tab for any of the costs.

It gets worse: House Republicans are currently con-templating paying for Hurricane relief and rebuilding the

Gulf Coast by drastic cuts in the main safety net programs for the poor. Nearly 40% of the proposed budget cuts will come from Medicaid, the Earned Income Tax Credit program, and money allocated for fighting AIDS in third world countries. At the same time, they propose going forward with more tax cuts for the rich and it is all but certain that most of the money spent for rebuilding will go into the pockets of fat cat developers and builders and businesses with political connections to the administration. This is redistribution with a vengeance—rebuilding the Gulf Coast and New Orleans on the backs of the poor.

Does the aftermath of Katrina have to turn out this way? Perhaps saner heads will prevail or the usually feckless Democrats will be able to override Republican callousness. For many of the people who witnessed the plight of those of our fellow citizens trapped in New Orleans as the flood waters rose, anger gave rise to the hope that the events of late August would rekindle compassion for the poor, that the obvious facts of life in New Orleans unveiled by Katrina would open the door to a reconsideration of race and poverty in America. Some have suggested that New Orleans might become a shining example of what could be done to improve the lives of all its citizens, not just the wealthy few, some of whom already envision a new New Orleans cleansed of poor people.

Justice will not be served unless New Orleans and the Gulf Coast are rebuilt in a way that benefits all its citizens and that will not happen without a struggle. Nor will the lessons of Hurricane Katrina hold without an effort to instill them in the minds of our fellow citizens. Americans' views of race and poverty are structured by a strange duality. The compassion and generosity that pours forth after a "natural" disaster or an unfortunate accident evaporates when faced with the quotidian realities of abject poverty. The true causes of poverty, *which are beyond the control any individual poor person*— residential segregation, poor schools, inadequate access to jobs, health care, and other public services—disappear only to be replaced by a cultural syndrome that ascribes poverty to the usual suspects: single-parent families, laziness, a proclivity for criminal behavior. All of these opinions reflect a judgment that poverty, especially Black poverty, is a consequence of bad individual choices, a "pathological" response to one's environment. Amazingly, some conservatives responded to Katrina's devastation by trotting out the specter of the "underclass," warning that it has not disappeared. Even liberal poverty researchers were not immune. Some of them think that the main task after Katrina is to study the fate of those displaced from New Orleans by the Hurricane to discover if "mobility" improves their economic opportunities.

Of course these sentiments are evasions. Such cultural ways of thinking are not easily dislodged; they seem impervious to logic and reason. But Katrina may provide an opportunity to take a few cracks at them and sound the moral tocsin that is necessary to attack the injustices of this society. But that is all it is: an opportunity. Disasters never usher in reform; the scales will not fall from people's eyes just because of Katrina or the despicable treatment of those of our fellow citizens trapped in the city. Instead, we will have to roll up our sleeves and work to make certain that the memories of Katrina are not forgotten.

21

Katrina and the Dutch Flood Disaster of 1953

*Eduard van de Bilt
and Johanna Kardux*

For weeks in September 2005, Katrina was headline news throughout Europe, but few people can have followed the news updates of the hurricane's aftermath with the same absorption as the Dutch. What was perhaps most surprising to Dutch television viewers in the early stages of the disaster was that, though predicted, the breaking of the levees which led to massive loss of life and property in New Orleans seems to have happened almost surreptitiously, outside camera reach. In the Netherlands, a country that derives its name from the fact that more than half of its land territory is below sea level, we're very familiar with prime time news images of chains of soldiers and volunteers valiantly passing on sandbags to weak spots in river dikes to prevent flooding of one of the three great rivers (the Rhine, Meuse and Waal) that have their estuary in the country. The one time that, as in New Orleans, the water came like a thief in the night, however, is deeply ingrained in Dutch public memory.

More than fifty years ago, a hurricane-force storm hit the Dutch west coast in the night of Saturday, January 31 to Sunday, February 1, 1953, battering the country for twenty-three hours. The storm was at its worst on Sunday morning at 4 AM, when it was accompanied by a spring tide of four to five meters high; a second, even higher spring tide followed in the late afternoon on Sunday. In the southwestern part of the country, dozens of dikes were destroyed and hundreds of others breached. Almost half of the province of Zeeland, the entire southwestern coastal area of the province of South-Holland, and the western reaches of the province of North-Brabant—some 2000 square kilometers—were flooded. Though a heavy storm had been predicted, due to the rudimentary communications systems of the time virtually all people in the afflicted areas were surprised in their sleep by the massive wall of water that swept away everything before it. 1,835 people were drowned, of whom 152 bodies were never found. Tens of thousands of houses and other buildings were destroyed or severely damaged. Moreover, according to the official government estimate, 25,000 cows, 140,000 poultry, and more than 1,500 horses died in the deluge, destroying the source of income of thousands in this largely rural area. Though in Dutch public memory the event is recorded as the Flood of 1953, survivors and their descendants still remember it simply as "the disaster."

It should come as no surprise, then, that the first televised images of the flooded streets of New Orleans and other coastal areas of Louisiana that reached the Netherlands immediately triggered collective and personal memories of the Flood of 1953, whose fiftieth anniversary was elaborately commemorated in 2003. The pictures of survivors on rooftops and in trees in Louisiana brought back family memories that haunted the childhood of one of the authors of this article, even though she herself was born after the disaster: the story of an aunt and uncle, who, together with their two small children and the uncle's aging parents, were rescued from the roof of their house in a small village on the island of Tholen, which was entirely flooded. Their good fortune was to live in one of the tallest houses in the village; even a decade later the water marks were still visible on the wall above the second-story windows.

Because the communication lines with the rest of the country were largely destroyed and roads, railway tracks, and other parts of the infrastructure were damaged in all the coastal provinces, the first rescue efforts were organized locally by individual citizens, while reinforcement of dikes in areas that had not yet flooded was organized by local mayors and aldermen, as well as by the local authorities responsible for water management. Among the first rescuers to arrive on the scene on Sunday evening were fishermen from the island of Urk, an orthodox Calvinist community located on the east side of the IJsselmeer, whose fishing fleet was anchored near the disaster area and who decided for once to violate the Sabbath to rescue people from rooftops, trees, and other higher locations such as the dunes while the storm was still raging. They were also the first to make contact with the navy, the Red Cross, and the national department of water management. It was not until Monday, February 2 that the scale of the disaster became known, and on Tuesday a national relief effort went underway. The Dutch army was mobilized, and since the Dutch military reportedly owned only one helicopter, US helicopters stationed in Western Europe contributed to the rescue and relief efforts, as did the German government.

More than 70,000 people had to be evacuated from the stricken areas. Dutch citizens volunteered en masse to take up the evacuees in their homes, though not all with charitable purposes: there are reports that some evacuees were used for cheap labor, doing household chores and filling regular jobs. A national disaster relief fund was established to aid the victims. According to one report, the equivalent of four billion euros was collected for the relief effort. So many goods were donated that the donation had to be stopped. The Dutch royal family played a prominent role in the response to the flood. Queen Juliana already made her first visit to the edge of the disaster area, the Krimpenerwaard in South-Holland, on Sunday afternoon, while her mother, former Queen Wilhelmina, visited with evacuees the next day after the storm had abated, setting a pattern of royal presence for future disasters of a national scope. The royal yacht was turned into a hospital ship and sent to the area, and room was made for the evacuees in the royal palaces of Soestdijk and Het Loo. A year after the event, about 5,000 people still had not been able to return home, and the disaster stimulated emigration to countries such as Australia and Canada.

Despite surface similarities between the aftermath of Katrina and the Dutch Flood of 1953, the historical contexts of the two events were vastly different. In 1953, the Netherlands was a nation under reconstruction; in 2005, the United States was a nation with a Federal government in disrepair. Eight years after the end of Nazi occupation of the country and with some of its major cities such as Rotterdam severely damaged by wartime bombing, the Dutch were rebuilding their nation. Under the inspired leadership of Prime Minister Willem Drees, a revered social-democratic statesman who was lovingly called "Father" Drees, and benefiting from economic aid through the Marshall Plan, the Dutch government was laying the foundation of the modern Dutch welfare state in the early 1950s. In view of these major projects of national reconstruction that were well underway when the Flood of 1953 hit, it was self-evident that the national government was responsible not only for repairing the damage, but also for the prevention of future floods of this scale. By October 1953, the dikes were sealed and flooded polders drained. The government immediately appointed a committee that within the year came up with a plan to strengthen the flood defences and cut the coastline by some 450 miles. Approved by parliament in the Delta Act of 1957, the Delta Project aimed to reduce the coast line by closing off four tidal inlets in the delta area and to raise all flood defences to so-called delta level, five metres above AOD (Amsterdam Ordnance Datum, mean sea level as defined for Amsterdam).

The ambitious multi-year project posed an enormous challenge: nowhere in the world had tidal inlets of the size and depth of those in the Dutch delta area been closed off before. Coordinated by the special national water management institute, *Rijkswaterstaat*, Dutch engineers and scientists of the Department of Marine Technology at Delft University of Technology successfully developed new, innovative technologies that brought about a revolution in hydraulic engineering. Seven huge storm surge barriers were constructed between 1958 and 1971. Work on the most ambitious part of the Delta project, a six-mile-long dam closing off the Easter Scheldt sea arm, started in 1967, but was halted in 1973 under pressure by environmentalists, the fishing industry, and scientists. The unique ecosystem of the Easter Scheldt, a breeding ground for fish and rich source of food for all kinds of wildlife, as well as a site for mussel and oyster farming, would be destroyed if the dam were to turn the saltwater inlet into a freshwater lake. A fierce public debate ensued, particularly in the southwestern provinces where the Flood of 1953 was vividly remembered, but in the end a compromise was reached that satisfied both environmentalists and those foremost concerned with safety. In 1975 the government decided to construct a huge storm surge barrier, with sliding gates that would remain open to the North Sea under normal conditions, but would be closed when water levels were unusually high or exceptionally heavy storms were predicted. Approved by parliament in 1978, designed by Dutch engineers, and built by a consortium of Dutch contractors, the Easter Scheldt storm surge barrier was completed in 1986, an epic feat of hydraulic engineering. The Delta Project as a whole was finally completed in 1997, with the construction of the Maeslant Barrier in the

New Waterway, which enables ships to enter the port of Rotterdam, but which has gates that can be closed to protect the city against flooding during heavy storms. The total cost of the Delta Project was about five billion euros, paid from taxes and national gas resources. The Delta Works, a truly exceptional mega-project that can serve as an international model for successful cooperation between public and private sectors, gave a huge impetus to both technological innovation and the economic development of a nation that had to rebuild itself after World War II, and is now facing the challenges of the twenty-first century.

According to Dutch experts interviewed after Katrina, the chance that the levee system protecting New Orleans would collapse if the city was hit by a hurricane was comparable with the situation in the Netherlands in 1953, when, too, the dikes were neglected. However, this risk level would have been totally unacceptable to the Dutch now: after the completion of the Delta Project, the chance of flooding by the sea of the southwestern region of the Netherlands has been reduced from once in eighty years in 1953 to once in 4,000 years now (for the rest of the Dutch west coast once in 10,000 years). Because of the traditional emphasis on individual responsibility the Federal and state governments in the United States are much less inclined to take long-term (and costly) collective preventive measures such as the Delta Works than the Dutch government, with its tradition of state responsibility and regulation. Rather than investing in a Mississippi Delta Project, the US authorities focus on damage control instead of protection and on limiting individual damage by, for example, private insurance. Local leadership and private initiative, the ideological mainstays of the neo-conservative Federal government, turned out to be totally inadequate in setting up rescue efforts and dealing with the chaotic aftermath of Katrina. An important difference is that in 1953 the Netherlands was still a socially and ethnically homogeneous society, particularly in the flooded rural areas, while Katrina exposed the glaring inequality and racial divide in American society in general, and in a big city like New Orleans in particular. Considering preventive evacuation the responsibility of individual citizens and local authorities, the authorities did not take into account that large groups in the poverty-stricken disaster area simply lacked the means of transportation to leave on time.

The United States can learn a lesson from the Dutch response to the Flood of 1953, but Katrina has functioned as an opportunity for critical self-reflection to the Dutch as well. Scientists predict that the chance of flooding will dramatically increase as an effect of global warming: rising sea levels (7 inches in the past century, with a predicted rise of 4 to 30 inches per century predicted for the future) may make the Delta Works in the long run inadequate, while the melting glaciers and increased rainfall increase the chances of flooding of the rivers in the inland areas, as happened several times in the past couple of decades. A combination of gale-force winds and high water levels in the rivers could prove fatal. Moreover, plagued by interethnic tensions and growing social disparities, the Netherlands too may face problems similar to those of New Orleans if a calamity such as flooding occurs in one of the big cities, Dutch disaster experts warn. Finally, in the past few years Dutch politics has taken a conservative turn, and Dutch politicians have increasingly taken over the rhetoric and policy of deregulation, decreased government intervention, and stimulation of private enterprise according to the American model. Katrina's exposure of an American government in disrepair should stand as a cautionary tale to the Dutch: in a time of natural disaster it's not wise to rely on Hans Brinker, that truly American invention and mythic figure of private, local initiative.

References:

The Delta Project: For Safety, Wildlife, Space and Water. The Hague: Ministry of Transport, Public Works and Water Management, 2001.

Jonkman, S. N. and J. K. Vrijling. "Nederland kan leren van New Orleans," *NRC Handelsblad*, September 1, 2005.

Rosenthal, Uri. "Katrina prikt mythen over rampen door," *Trouw*, September 10, 2005.

Rozendaal, Simon. "Katrina, Juliana, and Wilhelmina: Lessons from the Dutch Deluge of 1953," *Opinion Journal*, September 11, 2005.

Stichting Onderwijs Goeree Overflakkee, "Sporen van het woedende water." www.onwijsnat53.nl/WoedendWater/ (viewed October 2005)

"Watersnoodramp 1953," www.kustgids.nl/1953/fr_index.html?/1953/main.html (Viewed October 2005).

Web site of the Zeeland Archives, "De strijd tegen het water." www.zeeuwsarchief.nl/strijdtegenhetwater (viewed October 2005).

22

The Advantages of "Higher Ground"

Heather E. Bullock

Katrina's differential impact on Gulf Coast residents vividly illustrates how race and class privilege shape every aspect of daily life in the United States, even how natural disasters are experienced. Although hurricanes and storms are typically viewed as indiscriminate "levelers," the man-made disaster that ensued after Katrina hit land reveals the protective aspects of wealth and Whiteness. While thousands of low-income African Americans fled their low-lying homes in search of safety, with those fortunate enough to survive, warehoused in dangerous, unsanitary conditions, New Orleans's predominantly white, "old-line" families remained ensconced in their "higher ground" neighborhoods and if necessary, were whisked to safety via privately chartered airplanes (Cooper, 2005). With much of the city plunged into darkness, without safe drinking water or passable streets, the wealthy white residents of the Uptown area powered their homes with generators, hired private guards to keep their homes safe, and had fuel and fresh water delivered to them (Cooper, 2005).

In this all too familiar "tale of two cities," the stark contrast between the haves and have-nots is impossible to deny. Those without economic and social power lost everything; in some cases even their lives, when they could not access the most basic medical care. Meanwhile the wealthiest New Orleans residents, in spite of the turmoil around them, enjoyed afternoon cocktails with ice (Cooper, 2005).

Relatively little media attention has been directed toward understanding the buffer that protected higher-ground New Orleans residents from the ravages of Katrina. Instead, media reports have focused on high rates of poverty and unemployment among people of color; but such inequalities cannot exist in isolation. Great poverty cannot exist without great wealth. Nor can racial disadvantage exist in the absence of racial advantage.

The deep-rooted inequities made visible by Katrina, albeit news to some, are neither new nor invisible. The disparate impact on New Orleans residents is foreshadowed in national statistics on race and poverty and the widening income gap, showing these horrific events for what they are—a microcosm of broader, pervasive injustices. Every day millions of people of color, particularly those in female-headed households, live in poverty, go hungry, are denied medical treatment, and live in substandard housing, while the wealthy prosper at their expense. These extremes not only go unquestioned, they are widely accepted as legitimate reflections of merit. Our long history of viewing poverty as a vice and wealth as a virtue neutralizes social inequities, making it acceptable to demonize the poor and privilege the wealthy. In Katrina's wake, racist scapegoating was evident in news reports that emphasized "lawlessness," "looting," and the "stubbornness" of those who remained in their homes instead of focusing on why so many people were without water, food, or transportation to safety in the richest nation in the world.

The question now is whether we, as a nation, will ignore the structural sources of poverty and wealth or face them head on. Those who are advantaged by current economic policies are likely to prefer that Katrina signal nothing more than the need for a new FEMA director and a better emergency response system. These surface-level changes protect the advantages of those on higher ground, diverting attention away from the need for real living wages, the repeal of tax breaks for the wealthy, and the implementation of racially just policies. Indeed, some members of Congress are reportedly calling for budget cuts to programs that assist low-income groups (e.g. Medicaid and food stamps) to offset hurricane-related expenses, placing the burden of paying for Katrina on the backs of the poor (Center on Budget and Policy Priorities, 2005). We must demand otherwise.

References

Center on Budget and Policy Priorities (October 6, 2005), "Getting serious about deficits? Calls to offset hurricane spending miss the point; balanced set of first steps toward fiscal discipline needed." Retrieved October 10, 2005, from www.cbpp.org/10-6-05bud2.htm

Cooper, C. "Old-line families escape worst of flood and plot the future." *The Wall Street Journal,* September 8, 2005, A1, A12.

23

Empower the Poor
or the Fire Next Time[1]

Grace Lee Boggs

1

Hurricane Katrina gives us another opportunity to take a hard look at ourselves and begin the reordering of priorities necessary to prevent recurring natural, social, and political disasters like 9/11, the Iraq War, and New Orleans. The fury of Katrina, followed by the racist, classist, and subhuman herding of the Black, poor, and elderly into the Superdome and Convention center, leaving them without food, air, water, and toilets, and to war against one another, while government officials at all levels (including Blacks) ran around like Keystone Kops, has created a crisis of Biblical and constitutional proportions. We must seize this opportunity to ask ourselves and one another, "Why has this happened? Where do we go from here?"

---

[1] This essay is adapted from two of Grace Lee Boggs's articles, "The Fire Next Time" and "Empower the Poor" in the *Michigan Citizen* September 18–24, and October 2–8.

Forty years ago, Martin Luther King, Jr., agonizing over the twin disasters of the Vietnam War and the urban rebellions, called for a radical revolution of values. Our technological development has outrun our spiritual development, he warned. Moreover, we have lost our sense of community, of interconnection, and participation. To regain these, we must struggle not only against racism, but against militarism and materialism. We must, said King, begin a rapid shift away from a "thing-oriented society" to "a person-oriented one." King advised that we need to create programs that provide young people with opportunities to engage in self-transformation and structural change through direct action "in our dying cities."[2]

But King was assassinated on April 4, 1968, and since then few people have paid serious attention to his warnings. Instead most Americans, among them many Blacks and Democrats, are supporting, rather than opposing, rapid technological/economic development leading to the crises of global warming and the widening of the chasm between haves and have-nots. On the Gulf Coast, such development has meant the expansion of petrochemical and shipping industries to the detriment of now eroded wetlands and marshes which were natural barriers to disastrous flooding. It has also meant allowing New Orleans to become a city with a 28% poverty rate, and one of the country's highest murder rates, mostly in poor neighborhoods. Such negative consequences are extensions of what we see around the world, with multinational corporations in the global north that are systematically impoverishing people and environment, communities and cultures.

Today there are hundreds of thousands of evacuees from Hurricane Katrina who need compassionate assistance in the form of good housing, schooling, and medical care. Clearly elementary services like electricity, water, and sewer systems

---

[2]Martin Luther King, Jr. *Where do We Go From Here: Chaos or Community?* New York, Harper and Row, 1967.

need to be restored. But while meeting these emergency needs, we cannot afford to keep ignoring the fundamental questions raised by the Vietnam War, the urban rebellions in the 1960s, and by 9/11 only a few years ago. For example, if there is rebuilding, on what values should New Orleans be built? What is going to keep us from re-creating the culture of violence and dog-eat-dog that turned the Superdome into hell? Why can't we start involving our young people from kindergarten through twelfth grade in self-transforming and structure-transforming community-building programs along the lines proposed by Martin Luther King, thereby creating a culture of cooperation that will bring the neighbor back into neighborhood and also provide greater safety in times of natural disasters?

Who is going to ask and who is going to decide these questions?

These are the times to grow our souls. Otherwise, the fire next time.

2

"If you want to eliminate poverty, you have to empower the poor, not treat them as beggars."

This advice from Venezuelan President Hugo Chavez, offered during an interview with Amy Goodman on the "Democracy Now" program while he was in New York for a UN meeting, is as timely as the oil that Venezuela will soon start delivering at below-market prices to poor communities and schools in the United States. Unlike liberal Democrats and most US radicals, Chavez views the elimination of poverty not as something that governments promise to do *for* people, but as a participatory process through which people transform themselves and their reality simultaneously. This is also how Martin Luther King, after being confronted with the urban rebellions in the last three years of his life, began viewing the struggle against poverty.

Chavez described the process by which Venezuelans are currently struggling to eliminate poverty. In poor neighborhoods all over the country, thousands of people join Urban Land Committees. These committees draft a map of their neighborhood, then go house by house, family by family, assessing the problems, e.g. lack of running water, the condition of the houses, number of children, and available health care. Using financial and technological resources and equipment provided by the government, they interact with various technical commissions on water, energy and electrical supplies, etc. It is "a beautiful task we are conducting," Chavez said, "because we are trying to create a new model of democracy which is not only representative but participatory, a government that, as Abraham Lincoln already said, is of the people, by the people, and for the people." Such a government, says Chavez, is one that "transfers power to the people, especially the poorest of the poor."

Why can't we in the United States, who really want to eliminate poverty and not just talk about it, embark on a similar "beautiful task"? Everything else we have tried has failed. We could start by setting up neighborhood committees made up of community residents and middle and high school students. After drafting a map of the neighborhood, these intergenerational committees could also go house to house, assessing problems involving residents, and working with organizations that have the technical resources to be of help. Imagine how much both adults and young people would be empowered through this process of intergenerational activity; how much they would learn about their own realities from each; how many new and imaginative ideas and hopeful self-confidence would be generated, as they began to address seemingly insurmountable problems, while being transformed from victims into self-governing citizens!

A few days after listening to the Chavez interview I watched a telecast of the Town Meeting convened by the Congressional Black Caucus to discuss the poverty exposed to a wider public by Hurricane Katrina. The meeting consisted mainly of Black politicians rising either to be applauded or to appeal to their constituents to march and mobilize to empower these political figures in Washington. It all seemed very progressive. But I couldn't help thinking that as the number of Black representatives has increased in the last forty years so has the poverty rate. That is because we are still stuck in the same old minimalist "for the people" form of representative democracy. We have not accepted the challenge of the more complete proposition "of the people, by the people, and for the people" enunciated by Lincoln and continued by Martin Luther King, Jr.

Chavez's advice, coming at this time when Hurricane Katrina is forcing even George W. Bush to talk about "eliminating poverty," provides us with an unprecedented opportunity to make this leap in our thinking and practice.

24

Hurricane Katrina:
God and Social Morality

Rabbi Michael Lerner

It didn't have to happen.

And it didn't have to result in so many deaths and social chaos.

Before going down the route of spiritual analysis, let me pause for a moment of prayer and sadness for the suffering of the people of New Orleans and the Gulf, prayers for comfort of those who are mourning losses, and prayers for the survival of those who are still in danger. Prayer must always be accompanied by acts of *tzedaka*, righteousness or charity. The American Red Cross is playing a lead support role here, so you might consider donating to them.

But this is a classic case of the law of karma, or, what the Torah warns of, environmental disaster unless we create a just society, or what others call watching the chickens come home to roost, or what goes around comes around. Environmentalists are making a strong case that the escalated number and ferocity of hurricanes is a direct product of global warming, caused in large part by the reliance on fossil fuels. The persistent refusal of the United States to join the nations of the world in implementing the Kyoto Accords emission limits, and to impose serious pollution restrictions on the cars being sold in the United States, is a major factor in global warming. The development of housing and commercial structures, combined with massive oil and gas investments, destroyed the natural protections from storms that the coastal wetlands have previously provided.

Funds that were specifically allocated for New Orleans, which could have been used for rebuilding levees and storm protection, were cut from the Federal budget so that President Bush could use those resources to wage war in Iraq. Or the poor and the homeless in northern cities were told that "if they worked harder or had better habits or were smarter they'd have employment and wouldn't have to depend on others' help." Or the suffering of others was seen as "the hand of God."

And yet the law of karma or Torah doesn't work on a one-to-one basis, delivering "just rewards" to those who have been directly involved in causing evil. The terrible truth is that it is the *poor*, the *most vulnerable*, who are the first to suffer. The wealthy built their homes on higher ground, had better information, more insurance, and more avenues of escape. So, whether it is in facing the global warming–induced rising waters of Bangladesh or Malaysia or Louisiana or Mississippi, it's going to be "the least among us" who will suffer most immediately. That is why it is inappropriate to blame the victim: because the way the world has been created, the consequences of past social injustice, war and ecological irresponsibility come to a whole planet—because from the cosmic perspective we are one, we are all interdependent. So those who suffer the most are rarely those most culpable. It is the same with environmental cancers. It's often not the oil company executives, but poor people living in proximity to the air and water polluted by corporate irresponsibility; the corporations are abetted by the lawmakers, who depend on corporate contributions, and pay them back by imposing the weakest possible environmental regulations.

When some Christian fundamentalists talk about these as signs of impending doom of the planet, they are laughed at as irrational cranks. It's true that these fundamentalists see no connection between the doom and the environmental irresponsibility that the politicians they support have brought us. But nevertheless, their perception that we are living "at the end of time" can't be dismissed by those of us who know that the life-support systems of this planet are increasingly in danger if politics continues the way it has been going, with politicians in *both* parties capitulating regularly to the ethos of selfishness and materialism that is sustained by our corporate plunderers while being validated by the votes of many ordinary citizens.

Yet the fundamentalist message is deeply misleading as well; it seems to suggest that all of this is out of our hands, part of some divine scheme. But it's not. The Biblical version is quite different from what they say: it insists that the choice between life and death is in our hands. After laying out the consequences of abandoning a path of justice and righteousness, the Torah makes it clear that it is up to us. *Choose life*, it tells us. That choosing of life means trans-forming our social system, in ways that neither Democrats nor Republicans have yet been willing to consider, into a system based on love and caring, kindness and generosity, ethical and ecological responsibility, with awe and wonder at the grandeur of the universe replacing a narrow utilitarian approach to Nature. This is precisely what we have been calling for in our Interfaith organization, the Tikkun Community, and in our new project, the Network of Spiritual Progressives. We need a New Bottom Line—a fundamental transformation of what we value in this society. We want to take that message into the public sphere, into the political parties, into the media, into the schools, into the corporations.

There is one beautiful thing that sometimes happens during emergencies like this: the cynical realism that teaches us that people just care about themselves, a teaching that makes most of us feel scared to be "too generous" or "too idealistic" temporarily falls away, and people are allowed to be their most generous and loving selves. When the restraints are momentarily down, there is a huge outpouring of love, generosity and kindness on the part of many Americans. People do things like the example I saw yesterday: advertising on the internet's Craig's List that they are willing to take into their own homes for many months a family that has been displaced by the floods. This kind of selflessness is something that people actually yearn to let out, but under ordinary circumstances they would fear to do so. So watch the goodness show itself.

For me, this is a prayerful moment, entering the period just before the Jewish High Holidays (starting October 3), realizing that the Jewish tradition of taking ten days of reflection, repentance, and atonement is so badly needed not just by Jews, but by everyone on the planet. I hope we can find a way to build this practice among secular as well as religious people because America, indeed the whole world, so badly needs to *stop* and reflect, repent, and atone, and find a new way, a new path, and return to the deepest truths of love, kindness, generosity, nonviolence, and peace.

But it is also a moment for decisive action. So we in the Tikkun Community are calling on the US Congress and President Bush to launch a massive Domestic Marshall Plan to rebuild New Orleans; to provide upgraded housing for the poor of all of America's inner cities; to upgrade the social support infrastructure of those cities (including hospitals and emergency care facilities), and to provide catastrophe insurance for all lower income Americans.

Unfortunately, Democrats have been far too timid in responding to the failures of the Bush administration, concentrating their critiques on the competence of the

Federal response but largely ignoring the underlying class and race issues that systematically place the poorest and most vulnerable at the highest risk. Without strong intervention on behalf of the poor, the reconstruction and resettlement efforts will again be tilted in ways that are insensitive to the most vulnerable. We've already seen this process begin: people being moved from New Orleans into cities where they are given priority access to underfunded city services, thereby pushing the poor and homeless of those cities out of the already inadequate services available. Rather than pit these new victims against the victims of past injuries (including the injuries inflicted by downturns in the economy and relocation of jobs overseas), we need a comprehensive plan to eliminate domestic poverty.

We are calling for the first installment of $80 billion, comparable to the latest supplemental for the war in Iraq. If we gave $80 billion a year for each of the next five years to fund the reconstruction of New Orleans, giving a priority to providing low-cost but high-quality housing for the poor and homeless of that city, and to funding a massive housing and infrastructure reconstruction of all our inner cities, then we will have taken an important step toward our moral obligations as a society. This would put meaning behind the Biblical injunctions to care for the poor and powerless.

The Tikkun Community has already been involved in encouraging its members to donate funds and volunteer time to help the flood victims. Our concern, however, is that all the beautiful caring energies will be directed solely at dealing with immediate crisis (a very important thing to do) and miss the opportunity to address the larger societal changes that are needed and might actually be accomplished if we were to mobilize attention to rectifying the poverty that made this flood so costly in human lives. Americans are generous, but our government is not wise, and needs the pressure of ordinary citizens to get redirected. Just as we needed a New Deal to get out of the Depression, and not just individual donations to the poor, so today we need a massive societal effort to end poverty as well as rebuild New Orleans. The Domestic Marshall Plan is a first, but not full step toward addressing this issue.

25

Thinking for Ourselves: Fundamental Questions

Sharon Howell

There are moments that grab our hearts. Times when we have to face the consequences we have tried to ignore. The suffering of the people of New Orleans is such a moment. It is the most devastating experience for America in the lifetimes of most of us. We have seen death and suffering on an unimaginable scale. We have seen the collapse of government as children and elders died for want of water and care. And we have seen the deep divisions of race and class ripped open and brought to the center of public consciousness.

There are now so many fundamental questions we have to face. People all across the country are asking, "Who are we as a people? How did this happen in America? Is this the best we could do? Is this the kind of land we have become? Why? What can we do? How do we help one another?" Facing these questions will change us as a nation. If we approach them honestly, with open hearts and minds, we may become a better country, a people who will allow tragedy to enlarge our hearts. If, as so many in positions of authority would like, we turn away from them, we risk losing our souls.

Until Hurricane Katrina flattened the city as surely as a bomb attack, many in America persisted in the belief that nature is controllable. We acknowledged that other places, less sophisticated, developed or techno-savvy, suffered from floods, earthquakes and tidal waves.

But not us.

Until now.

Now we know that all our tampering and tinkering cannot withstand the awesome powers of wind and water. And now many more of us are coming to believe that these powers, rubbed raw by the abuse and neglect of our earth for centuries, are becoming more intense.

Those who urged international agreements to protect and preserve our world have argued in vain that we are altering our climate in ways that are making it harsher and less forgiving. They have warned of the deepening crisis created as forces of nature are stretched beyond their capacity to support life. They have warned that flood and drought will intensify if we continue to ignore our responsibilities to the earth.

We have seen the truth of these statements in faraway places, but somehow, we have managed to pretend that America would be immune. And so we have continued to live with little regard for the earth on which we depend for life. We have elected leaders who have withdrawn from every single international effort to reverse this devastation and who are systematically dismantling decades of efforts to preserve and protect our land, water and air.

Katrina is the first serious storm in our lifetimes to break through this denial. But she will not be the last. She gives us the opportunity to look with honesty and humility at what we have wrought and to begin the slow, necessary process of restoring balance to our ways of living. Such reassessment means thinking not only about our relationships to the earth, but to one another. We are living with leaders who believe the only purpose of government is to provide a good business climate. But government is a sacred covenant among people.

Through governance we take collective actions to secure the essential elements of life. Government is the fundamental means we have to express our common, best hopes. New Orleans has shown us the horrific consequences of a view of government that is destroying the fabric of our country. It is a cry for change.

26

'Ike Kupaianaha

Now that it has been witnessed

Manulani Aluli Meyer
Native Hawaiian

Aloha is the intelligence with which we meet life.
—Olana Kaipo Ai

We have seen it. It has been witnessed. *Truth is a continuum of understanding and a capacity to comprehend.*[1] The point is this: Do we *understand* the truth of New Orleans? Do we *comprehend* the truth of war? There is no time to doubt our clarity here—none at all. From all biological, social and environmental indicators on this planet, it is clear to many we have only a short space within which to act. Do you *know* this? Are you ready to enter a plan to shift our consciousness? Are we prepared to be fully uninhibited to *speak the word our mind thinks*[2] so that we enter the capacity of seer, prophet, and *noho* during these times of great, great need. Yes, we can

---

[1] David Hawkins, *The Eye of the I.* A treasure trove of truth and guidance for this time. Read his first book *Power vs. Force* before you read *The Eye of the I.*
[2] *Ibid.*

do it together. You who are reading—my aloha is present. Mahalo for being here. *There is a reason why you have picked this up.*

The Great Awakening: Intentionality Rising

> *Truth is the highest goal*
> *and aloha is the greatest Truth of all.*
> —Halemakua

New Orleans, 9/11, the war in Iraq, gas prices, warmer climate—all point to the obvious: the time is upon us to usher in the Great Awakening. It is encouraged by a beloved Maori elder who has written clearly and with calm conviction born from ancient knowing: *We must describe the higher at all times.*[3] It is the regenerative salve to bring conscious intentionality back into the core of how we will right what is completely mad in the world. Intentionality, defined in Buddhism as the "first movement of the mind toward an object . . . not necessarily deliberate or fully conscious"[4] helps frame this discussion. It is the illumination on our path we have to switch on with conviction, clarity and action. It will exorcise our own lethargy and return us to the awakened state we have always been in. You are a woman and man of your word, now become a being of your *intention.* This is what portends the awakening that must be *drawn forth* in ourselves, our families, our communities, our world. This is the essence within the word and idea of *educare*—or Education. And it must be the context we help ourselves and youth grow in. We must rescue what is most holy in our culture: our children, ourselves.

It will mean *radically* changing our Education systems. Are you ready to think through five simple ideas that will help you, your students, or your own children *see* what is going

---

[3]Maori Marsden. *The Woven Universe: Selected Writings of Rev. Maori Marsden.* Te Wananga o Raukawa (2003).
[4]Francesca Fremantle. *Luminous Emptiness: Understanding the Tibetan Book of the Dead.* Boston: Shambhala (2001).

on around us? Then we can respond effectively and reverse the trend that is so clearly out of control. Take heart, fear and doubt are merely the banks of a river. Courage and the power of love, joy and truth are forever at the center of life, but the banks *are* needed to pull the water forward.[5] Here, perhaps is the purpose of fear. It is like any other energy—something to note, something to learn from, something to approach as a mother approaches a child in agony. But it will never ultimately describe the river. We must take heart in what is the true nature of life and keep that as the lift in our step toward the change that is now upon us. Are you ready? We have much work to do. To un-do.

Five Ways to Awaken Education and Change the World

> *Be the change you wish to see in the world.*
> —Gandhi

1 That Literacy which makes Knowledge a Commodity will be the downfall of Western civilization —A Reading the World Alternative[6]

Literacy in its most common form makes knowledge a commodity—those with the most win. This is the society we have created. Derrida has convinced me that literacy will indeed wreak havoc within Western civilization. I would like to add a caveat: an *over-reliance* on literacy will be the demise. *Think about it.* I speak from experience that an over-reliance on the map does little to understand the territory of what life truly means. Literacy merely *points* to what can only be understood in experience. It is a tool to open minds, not a blunt object to lay waste to our children's dreams. Literacy

---

[5]This idea came from Nobel Laureate Rabindranath Tagore in the Indian classic *Sadhana*.

[6]Jacques Derrida, father of Deconstruction and respected world philosopher, believed that literacy would indeed implode Western culture because of its distance from consciousness and experience.

should expand into "reading the world" so that our future adults understand what they are looking at and do not recoil in lethargy and muteness at how to thus effect change.[7] Our children must *create* knowledge and know they are part of its legacy and not simply feel they are passive consumers of some form of it.

Literacy also privileges our left hemisphere of the brain, famous for sequencing, logic, and linear activities. Our world needs to see things differently now. We are in desperate need of both left- *and* right-brain doers, and gestalt thinkers who see wholeness in ideas, and work in new patterns of consciousness not yet detailed, because we have yet to encourage wide-range thinkers. We are dulling our children with the uniformity found in standardization and timed tests. We are drilling them on the lowest possible forms of our potential intelligence and it is affecting all future generations. If you have something, anything to do with schools, *stop* it now. Our children will learn to read in their own time. Uniformity of thinking has never worked before. Why on earth do we think it will work now? Make reading, writing and comprehending a joyful activity, not an exercise of competition, fear and self-ridicule.

2 Allow children to talk with each other!

When did school become a prison? Why do our children carry guns? I believe our schools mirror our society and our society mirrors our schools. Why not alter the future of our world by making learning a shared and relationship-building activity? *I mean it.* We will learn how to trust, communicate and speak to one another again. It is as simple as asking your students to "turn to your partner and share a highlight of the poem." Turning to our partners teaches us to respect what others have to say and draws forth what is best in us. I say this from experience. I am an idealist, not naïve, and I have

---

[7]"Reading the world" is an idea from Brazilian philosopher/educator Paulo Freire.

seen this work over and over and over again. Our youth are dying to share and be listened to. They run to class grateful for the opportunity to explore their own minds and exhibit what they know to be true: *true intelligence is self-knowledge* (Plato). Try it with your first-graders and with your seniors. It doesn't matter what age. We know that learning is a social process, even when we are doing it solo, it is always good to share a highlight of what we ourselves have come up with. Scaffold the idea first. Remember, our youth are trained to not trust, to compete with others, to doubt in the intelligence of another. We must believe they are their own best teachers to turn this around. We as adults must foster an intelligence of community and we must exhibit that in our own behaviors.

3 Erase competition between students and make learning a path toward inner excellence that is a shared phenomenon

This is not such a radical idea! We simply need to change our minds as to the purpose of Education, and the purpose of learning anything. Is it to beat someone? Is it really to be isolated, stingy and non-cooperative? When did learning become lethal; how on earth are we going to evolve in this planet when we teach our youth to cheat, cram, and to memorize fragmented facts unconnected to meaning. This translates as hatred for others' success, extreme privacy for our own small clicks and thus a non-caring populace foreign to basic democratic ideals.

Competition has its place. It cannot be the main motivation for how and why we learn, however. What I am discovering is that when kids feel safe, happy and productive, they are learning what cannot possibly be assessed in numbers. They are plugging into why they are alive—to joy in each other's company, to feel encouraged with their own evolutionary process, to drink in the peace of what it means to be in a group process excelling toward goofiness. This clearly cannot happen in overcrowded classrooms with one adult as the teacher. Our society is corrupted with the ignorance and bigotry we exhibit with regard to reform in Education. Of course this form of consciousness was shaped in a competitive classroom that heralded Darwin's theory as a way of life for our society. It is not the consciousness we must posit today. Survival of the fittest works to fracture what communal care, wise counsel and ancient paths to harmony can guide us toward. The strong will never ever stay on top forever. We know that what is coming is open, caring, wise. This is what I am learning from New Orleans.

4 Develop a pedagogy of Aloha[8]

Mahalo Dr. Ku Kahakalau! Ku spearheads our Hawaiian Charter School movement in Hawaiʻi and has put forth this idea that we must *teach with aloha*. It rings true with us as Native Hawaiians and we know our children skip to school because of it. Loving our children is the most vital aspect of how best to learn. It's not about love, it's about *loving*. Period.

Aloha makes our children and young adults smart. We recognize this in them and practice it within ourselves. We are committed to this, and yes, it can be a struggle for us as practitioners, but it is more often not recognized as something of value in our young American culture. This is why we as indigenous people are stepping up to the plate. We have seen this before. We have experience. It is in our stories and place names. We have survived lifetimes of the ebb and flow of greed, conquest, disease, tidal waves, eruptions, change. It is now time to refashion the value of what loving means. *Aloha is our intelligence.* It must be cultivated and encouraged as it brings out what is best about life. It is not corny or impossible. It is vital and necessary.

---

[8]The idea of pedagogy of Aloha came from the brilliant mind and relentless spirit of Dr. Ku Kahakalau, a visionary leader in our Hawaiian Charter School movement.

5 Bring land and water awareness back into our world

Land is our mother, Blackfoot elder Leroy Little Bear explained to an audience at Berkeley. He told me later that it was not a metaphor. It is the nature of our biggest disease—that we no longer see ourselves as earth, water, air and fire. They have become elements outside us and we have become their pollutants and their controllers. As all ancient cultures detail in mythic and esoteric terms: *We are that,* and that which we do to the world we do to ourselves.[9]

These ideas we learn. Why not teach them again in a ritualized deep way in our schools? Heaven knows they are not in our mainstream ethos in business, science or social studies. Greg Cajete teaches us that we must learn *from* land, not simply *about* land.[10] Here is a native way to re-enter relationship—not via intellectualization literacy privileges, but from the space of experience, knowing and intimacy. We must wake up with regard to the miracle of our environment and see us as part of the solution. This means that we must change our curriculum to care for lands and water around our neighborhoods. We must begin here again. It is called Place-Based pedagogy and it is as old as time. We must teach our children and ourselves to grow our own food, to replenish soil, to rethink all purchases so that recycling is the last resort. We must change our thinking of how we can sustain and nourish our environment, because if we do not care for this and believe it is expendable, we are in essence doomed. Here is the final point to this five-point star: *Malama Aina*— take care of our Mother. In doing so we are enlightened. And as beloved elder Halemakua has shared: *Enlightenment* is *the goal of Education.*

---

[9] Please see the 45-minute DVD *Suzuki Speaks.* He outlines these ideas clearly and with great graphics. Perfect for any classroom (biology, English, political science, science, history, etc.).

[10] Greg Cajete, *Native Science.*

Haʻina mai ka puana

The story is told

Ulu aʻe ke welina a ke aloha

Aloha is the essence within the soul

These are the thoughts that came when thinking of New Orleans and the war in Iraq. I must tell the reader that I no longer read the newspapers and watch television. (It has been four+ years.) I have decided to no longer be influenced by mainstream media. I am working on getting myself into a different frequency, and my diet of images, ideas and commentary is now within specific places, books, friends, family and colleagues. I have seen only a handful of pictures of the atrocities and heard from friends and family about their own take of the experiences.

To the question of what I think about these world events—I have answered with my life. The focus of Education is my family's life work. As a Native Hawaiian in the thick of a world movement to reclaim knowledge systems that work to save our planet, minds and bodies, I have been privileged to be around indigenous practitioners and scholars who are completely and fully awake. What I am learning is this: we must take what is ancient and shape it into what is authentic. This means we must articulate an intelligence that once again cares for this planet. That is key. Earth. Fire. Water. Wind. And because of that ancient practice of right relationship we will find ourselves back in safe harbor with land, sky, water, self and other. It is best summarized by our beloved Hawaiian *kupuna*, Halemakua:[11]

---

[11]Halemakua. Personal and unpublished writings (2004).

The educators who face the present world opportunity should see to it that a sound foundation is laid for the coming civilization; they must undertake that it is general and universal in its approach. They must lay an empathic importance upon those great moments in our ancestral history wherein man's divinity flamed forth and indicated new ways of thinking, new modes of human planning, and thus changed for all time the trend of human affairs.

27

The Aftermath
of Hurricane Katrina

Coming to grips with US failure

David Cohen

The United States is in a failing state mode. A US National Security strategy paper in 2002 concluded America is now threatened less by conquering states than by failing ones. Recent performance, or non-performance, by the US government shows us that our own government is a threat to our security as a people. Failed states are associated with the export of international terrorists, drug barons and weapons arsenals. That is dangerous enough. There are other attributes of failure that we ignore at our peril especially when we see our reflection in the mirror if we have the gumption to look at ourselves.

During and in the aftermath of the 2005 hurricanes of Katrina and Rita I was in Bosnia and Ukraine. I spoke with many in Bosnia who had lived through their savage conflict in 1992–95 when they went without water and food. In

Ukraine some of those I met with had participated in the Orange Revolution in 2004. Their parents and grandparents remember World War II and the Stalin-forced hunger of the 1930s.

My professional work has taken me to south and southeast Asia where I have spoken with colleagues and peers who have worked on tsunami recovery. They have given me a deeper understanding of what we can learn from disaster prevention and relief so that fewer lives will be lost in future disasters.

In addition I have discussed the impact of Katrina with community organizers and health professionals in our country. I come away angry and dismayed at officials at all levels of governance, including the Democrats. What encourages me is the extraordinary response of people on the ground in Louisiana and Mississippi. That strength is our resource to create an America where poverty ends and is not hidden from view.

This is not about Bush-bashing. Though it is deserved, it is too easy. Nor is it about our calling for Democrats to be Democrats. That requires social movements to gain political traction as they did in the civil rights, antiwar, women's and environmental movements. Our challenge is to create a politics that transforms the United States into a country that practices equality and justice.

I want to briefly discuss what it means to be a failing state, followed by how those outside of the United States saw us and what our next steps must be to become a whole people.

Failed States

The concept of "failed states" has been developed by the Fund for Peace and the Carnegie Endowment for International Peace, along with *Foreign Policy* magazine. When its criteria are applied, twenty states are in critical condition, twenty more are in danger of going into free fall, and twenty more are on the borderline. My work experience has brought me to eight of the states that are in critical condition or in danger of falling into that category. The criteria that decide whether a state is failed are based on twelve categories:

- demographic pressures
- refugees and displaced persons
- group grievances
- human flight
- uneven development
- economic decline
- consider the state as illegitimate
- weak public services
- violated status of human rights
- out-of-control or weak protective security apparatus
- factionalized elites
- external intervention

The eight states where I have worked that are in the category of failing or in danger of failing are: Bangladesh, Bosnia-Herzegovina, Ethiopia, Guatemala, Nepal, Sierra Leone, Ukraine and Zimbabwe. The United States cannot be compared to these states. But it is an act of arrogance to think we are exempt from failure. When it comes to Katrina we have abandoned our idea of American exceptionalism, We can no longer think of ourselves as a "city on the hill." In many parts of our country we have the same shameful economic conditions and environmental degradation that people in developing countries face. The United States in recent years has seen poverty grow. The careful Census Bureau reports that over 1.1 million people fell into poverty in 2004, bringing the total to 37 million. Louisiana and Mississippi are two of the three poorest states in our country (New Mexico is the third). What Katrina stripped bare were the invisible issues of class and race in the United States. That fear and hostility is what prompted Mississippi Governor Barbour's comment that looters, now acknowledged to be far fewer in number than at first sensationally reported, would be dealt with "ruthlessly." The Governor used a euphemism for "shoot to kill."

By any reasonable criteria, and based on what affected people experienced, state, local and especially the national government's official behavior and policies have been one of inaction and neglect. The US government failed to respond by sending troops and equipment in a timely way to advance the evacuation. That contrasts sharply with our effective response in the 1906 San Francisco earthquake. We have gone backwards as human services decline, and with such a decline people's economic and social rights are ignored and violated. These rights are recognized by most of the world. The United States refuses. We plainly do not respect the decent opinions of humankind.

As we examine the categories that describe failed states we learn that the US performance is shamefully dismal. We create an especially hard life for the over 20% of children living in poverty. The quality of our neonatal, prenatal and child care shows an absence of respect for human life. Since 2000 child mortality has increased in the United States. Inequalities in health financing and access to health care create a paradox: countries that spend less on health care than the United States have healthier populations. Group grievances fester, caused by the escalating income gaps between rich and poor. Our environmental neglect creates the need for human flight, as evidenced by Katrina. This leads to an internal refugee population that displaces our citizens from their homes and neighborhoods.

The evidence is clear. The United States is a failing state. Others see us that way as well.

How Do Others See Us?

We all believe a picture is worth a thousand words. The exception comes in what the President and his mother said. President Bush's statement, five days after Katrina struck, on his much delayed visit to the hurricane sites, that he could not anticipate "the breach of the levees" astounded Americans and the world. That showed he is an official who is not a Commander-in-Chief. The official ignorance was compounded by the President's mother statement about people in the Houston Texas stadium that "since so many of the people are underprivileged, this is working very well for them." To add to her grossness, she said "it is sort of scary" to think that "they all want to stay in Texas."

The President's and his mother's comments were constantly referred to by my Bosnian and Ukrainian colleagues and were noted in emails from Bangladesh, India and Indonesia. The Bosnians, who experienced the harshness of the war in Sarajevo for nearly four years, asked doesn't the President know that people cannot live without water and food. In our situation, they said, we found ways to help one another. Officials did not help the people of New Orleans. They stood by and watched. Ukrainians drew an instant parallel with Chernobyl. In Ukraine reactors were not upgraded, they said, in spite of multiple previous accidents. This was reinforced by an official culture of secrecy that is just now being challenged. We neglected our levees despite years of warnings that go back to the great Mississippi River flood of 1927. We made it worse by depleting our wetlands that gave New Orleans greater protection.

Similarly, many of my Asian peers warned that the domination of market mania causes environmental and social problems to worsen. A failure to correct the mentality of the market *über alles* sets the stage for the next disaster. Their experience stems from constantly facing cyclones and typhoons. All will remember the tsunami. Those with resources used the information to escape Hurricane Katrina, but not the poor. Even if they had received information, they were not in a position to act on it unless buses, vans and a volunteer corps of helpers were organized to help them. A friend from India noted most of the people hurt are people of color, so why should the Bush Administration "give a toss."

That leads to another critical matter: in Louisiana and Mississippi there was an absence of social cohesion that, if present, would have led to area-wide organization and response. Yes, there were fine examples of help after the hurricane from the voluntary, religious and relief sectors, but shockingly, there were almost no organized evacuation efforts by the government or civil society. In contrast, when the cyclones hit Bangladesh, rickshaw drivers and transport workers took people to the hospital and construction laborers organized food brigades for the victims. Tsunami relief workers and Indian senior civil servants have volunteered to come over and help us rebuild in ways that listen to people's voices. We face a test of maturity for us as a nation: can we accept such advice? Or will we reject it out of hand, as we did with the offer of help from competent Cuban doctors, who could have helped us deal with the dangerous health consequences of Katrina.

What Do We Do to Make It Better?

Clearly the United States has to stop failing. People in Ukraine and Bosnia spoke directly to me. They said when you cannot evacuate those in danger, or provide them food and water you are neither as powerful as you think you are or as caring and kind as you say you are.

How can we reject medical help?

In every respect we moved many rungs down the ladder of respect and power. Our vulnerabilities showed as much as they did on September 11. As a physician from Ukraine, a frequent visitor to the United States and an admirer of our country, told me: "You are all about show, and therefore you deny what is real."

We face reality best by looking at what our sources of strength are. Naomi Klein's trenchant journalism shows that our strength is in people and their ability to organize. In New Orleans today, and in Mississippi as well, there are vital community organizations that have been working to improve education, health, jobs and transportation. Richard Rhodes, the author of *The Making of the Atomic Bomb,* in a *New York Times* op-ed with Gwyneth Craven, astutely compared the wolves and feral dogs roaming the exclusion zone of Chernobyl with the contractors and lobbyists roaming Louisiana, Mississippi and Washington. Will community based organizations direct the rebuilding of New Orleans and environs or will it be Halliburton and other corporate carpetbaggers who worship only the almighty dollar? Organizations such as the Douglass Community Coalition, Community Labor United, the Stewpot Organization, and others like them should be in the driver's seat. Those who ignore history are destined to repeat it. In the context of the hurricane areas African Americans primarily, and poor people of any color, cannot count on any level of government to protect them. The community organizations have created their systems of accountability that, if given an opportunity, have the capacity to hold governments accountable and responsive while holding the rapacious interests at bay. Our priorities are distorted, as shown by the United States spending more on the military than all other nations combined. I see that as a vulnerability. (Certainly the insurgency in Iraq has shown how a small zealous group can inflict heavy losses on a great power.) There are other measures as well. We had better understand that the self-created placards on the roads from New Orleans begging food, water and medicine were a reproach to the United States, and not just to the President. It made sharply visible our deep racial and class divisions.

The need for Federal dollars distributed to support community ownership should be a given. There is bound to be a major political struggle to make this happen. There will even be a struggle to assure that our public investments are in people, to advance education, child care, food and nutrition. Surely we should make a start in dealing with global warming and taking far-reaching steps to protect wetlands. Clearly there is a need for infrastructure modernization that halts the years of neglect of our bridge, levee and transportation maintenance. These are all needed, and conflict directly with the Bush view. Nevertheless the issues should be sharply drawn with the Administration.

What else to do? More than ever the perspective has to be changed. That is why the authentic voices of community groups such as the Douglas Community Coalition have to be amplified. With such amplification, and added organization, the framework and perspective can be changed. What is needed is a politics of transformation, not a politics of interest-group brokering.

As New Orleans is rebuilt, let us draw on the exciting experience of Wake County in North Carolina. A policy of mixed-income education has dramatically improved reading skills of children from low-income families, primarily African-American and Latino. Community organizations working with day-laborer organizations can serve as the hiring halls for jobs that are needed in reconstructing communities. A savvy health worker told me that from her experience what saddened her the most about the effects of Katrina was that the people left behind lacked decent health care to begin with. How could they survive walking miles with heart conditions, high blood pressure, diabetes and obesity? She wrote me that "they were neglected people to begin with." That must end!

If we do not want to be vulnerable, then we have to control the rapacious forces eager to capitalize on the destruction and rebuilding: contractors, lobbyists, officials and those elites who want low-income communities to be excised from the community and political landscape. The penalties must be harsh and, as Mississippi Governor Barbour put it, "ruthlessly" applied. (I am betting that he did not mean it in this context.) The nonprofit sector has to also be an aggressive performer and not accept the crumbs from a visit with the President as gratification. Unless it organizes funds to amplify the voice of the poor and community groups so that they can set the public agenda, and sustain it, little will change for the better.

The need is for leadership, so that the United States meets its responsibilities as a state. National leadership has been close-minded in recognizing that parts of the United States are as poor as many countries located in the Southern Rim. We deny what is real. Leadership is called for which recognizes that we must pull together as a community and not leave any individual behind. A model of leadership can be drawn from Nehemiah, who rebuilt Judah and Jerusalem by working first with the people to protect their security and provide their basic needs. Nehemiah's leadership was exercised in cooperation with the people. The people were stakeholders and producers who created the community they came to love. That is a model for all of us to work towards. It is the path that will move the United States away from a failing state to one that meets it duties to its people.

28

Hurricane Katrina: Recipe for More Disaster or Hopeful Reconstruction?

Stan Oden

The Hurricane Katrina disaster exposed the social, political, and economic underbelly of decades of race and class oppression and governmental indifference to it in the United States. The destruction of large sectors of the African-American community of New Orleans represents not only the destructive power of a Category 4 hurricane, but the neo-conservative policies of decades of right-wing Republican domestic and foreign policies.

This disaster lays at our feet the consequences of the neo-conservative formulation of individualism, free market policies and foreign occupations, which have never benefited those individuals in poverty or who are in the working class. These policies began in earnest under the Reagan administration, but were actually foreshadowed by Richard Nixon in 1969, with Daniel Moynihan's suggestion that we treat the urban poor with "benign neglect." The eventual stripping of social programs, which were designed and operated by the affected populations themselves, was now part of the neo-conservative strategy to diminish the self-determination of urban residents. Programs evolving from the Great Society era had begun to address issues of housing, education, youth delinquency, unemployment, job training, drug prevention, and many other issues. From 1965 to 1980, programs focused on the urban and poor communities provided some hope, by outlining alternatives to urban renewal programs and social dislocation. Starting in 1980 under the Reagan administration and lasting for eight years, more than 30% of the grants-in-aid to state and local governments were cut (Judd and Swanstrom, 2002, p. 240). An additional 20% were cut when seventy-six categorical grant programs were consolidated into nine block grants (Judd and Swanstrom 2002, p. 240).

George Bush Sr. continued this onslaught on social programs, and promoted the false hope of "A Thousand Points of Light", although, as Cornel West reminds us, "You cannot use charity as justice" (speech at Shiloh Baptist Church, Sacramento, California, September 17, 2005). President Bill Clinton was faced with a Republican Congress led by Newt Gingrich's "Contract for America" (which was actually a contract *on* America), and saw hostility from a Republican majority in his first term. In his second term, he was confronted by a lynch-mob Republican Party that dimmed any hope of any substantive focus on issues of race and class. Clinton, to his credit, brought up the issue of racism, and found kindred spirits in recognizing the strength and vitality of the Black community, particularly through the Black church. However, Clinton's impeachment fiasco provided the needed ammunition for neo-conservatives, led by Karl Rove and George Bush, to steal the White House in 2000 with the disenfranchisement of thousands of Black voters in Florida, and to continue the neglect and deception of "compas-sionate conservatism." This "compassionate conservatism" has allowed for the number of persons in poverty to increase to 37 million. The Bush administration's tax cuts for the rich, along with the misadventures in Afghanistan and the destruction of Iraq, has siphoned off hundreds of billions of dollars to these theaters of war, and has sapped and drained the economic and social possibilities in the United States.

The tragedy of New Orleans, and other affected communities along the Gulf Coast, is that the social and physical dislocation of the lives of people who are already suffering from bad housing, unemployment, underemployment, and poor health became exacerbated. It is clear that this government refuses to bring, and is incapable of bringing, social and economic justice to the residents of New Orleans. The elimination of prevailing wage standards in the reconstruction of New Orleans opens the door to out-of-state employers and employment. The recent rescinding of no-bid contracts was a direct result of pressure put on the Federal government to stop the cronyism between corporations like Halliburton and the government for development projects. This tendency to bypass the democratic structures that will benefit all persons in New Orleans will doom the city to becoming an economic engine for the tourist and oil industries.

The need for a democratic economic reconstruction of New Orleans is desperately clear. What is needed is a reconstruction that trains and employs New Orleans residents in construction and urban development. Needed is a reconstruction that trains New Orleans residents in health-care services, which will help the city decentralize its health-care system in order to serve more people needing medical services. Also needed is a reconstruction that reorganizes the New Orleans police department, so that New Orleans residents can feel safe from marauding police officers, such as the ones who brutally beat a sixty-four-year-old New Orleans resident before television cameras five weeks after the hurricane. New Orleans residents need to feel safe from corrupt underpaid police officers who brutalize and harass the Black community. A citizens' review commission should be instituted to bring public accountability to the

New Orleans police department and New Orleans residents should be hired to help police their community.

The present reconstruction of New Orleans should not be in the hands of the crony-laden Bush White House. This task needs to be given to the residents of the Gulf Coast area, with democratic principles embedded in the allocation of resources, so that race and class do not become the influencing components in the decision-making process used in distributing assistance. In reality, only the removal of the neo-conservatives from power will offer real hope of any long-term reconstruction of New Orleans and the Gulf Coast.

The hurricane may have blown in a destructive force of wind and rain, but the heart, soul, beat and self-determination of the people of New Orleans will rise again, and we will all be the better for it.

References

Judd, Dennis, and Todd Swanstrom. *City Politics*, New York, Longman, 2002.

West, Cornel. Speech at Shiloh Baptist Church, Sacramento, California, September 17, 2005.

29

Katrina, New Orleans, and Intentional Neglect

Hardy T. Frye

> *"But I do know that it's true that if you wanted to reduce crime, you could, if that were your sole purpose, you could abort every Black baby in this country, and your crime rate would go down."*
>
> William Bennett (former US Secretary of Education and Drug Czar) went further to note that it would be "an impossible, ridiculous and morally reprehensible thing to do, but your crime would go down."
>
> —Eugene Robinson, October 4, 2005

Bennett's recently proposed "final solution" to reducing crime in America is a bold representation of a member of America's intellectual elite and a former high government official making clear racist statements and it provides a point of reference as we try to explain the nightmare that occurred in New Orleans when Hurricane Katrina struck, flooding the 67% Black community of New Orleans. Was the slow and inadequate reaction to this disaster by local, state and Federal officials because the city and the areas destroyed were predominantly Black, or was it because a significant number of these people were living in poverty? In either case, they were not major players in New Orleans and Louisiana politics—except on Election Day.

Was it both, race and class? Was the government's response at all levels extremely slow because of a "social climate" in this country promoted by significant members of the majority population, as articulated by William Bennett? Mr. Bennett's proposal is nothing short of a proposed genocide toward Black America.

Was what occurred in New Orleans a case of intentional neglect? By "intentional neglect" I mean the process put in place by several Republican administrations, starting with the Reagan administration, which amounts to a deliberate assault and dismantling of government programs that attempt to address America's poor, many of whom were Black Americans residing in major urban areas like New Orleans. I'm speaking of programs that attempted to rebuild the infrastructure within these communities, deliver services, and address the pressing employment needs of such communities. Programs that other levels of government had shown they were unable to provide to meet the growing needs of these communities. Did intentional neglect render the Federal government incapable of providing effective and timely responses? Lani Guinier, while discussing this matter in relation to the Bush administration's ability to react in New Orleans, suggested, " this is not just about poor Black people in New Orleans. This is about a social movement, with an administration that is bent on weakening the capacity of the national government to act" (Duke and Wiltz, 2005).

Could what occurred in New Orleans be characterized as racist acts by psychologically deranged or mean spirited whites at both the state and Federal level? Were "Black political leaders" under control of the white power structure of New Orleans? There is some evidence supporting such a speculation at this point, but not enough for an indictment, although some would disagree. Was Black political leadership serving as a proxy of the white power structure?

Many victims of this hurricane and many Blacks and whites outside New Orleans believe this to be the case. Several articles I have read suggested that the Mayor of New Orleans was strongly supported by the local white political elites. We do know that just days after Katrina struck, the Mayor was huddled in a Dallas, Texas hotel room meeting confidentially with white business leaders, including one who "has long advocated a thorough redevelopment (and cleaning up of crime in) the city." In this meeting there was reportedly discussion about "the triaging of poorer Black areas, and a corporate-led master plan for rebuilding the city" (Davis and Fontenat, September 30, 2005 and Cooper, September 8, 2005).

Naomi Klein, in her essay "Purging the Poor," interviewed Mark Drennen, President and CEO of Greater New Orleans Inc. and a top corporate lobbyist, who, one would suspect, is a major political figure in New Orleans's elite political circle. Klein noted that Drennen ". . . was in an expansive mood, pumped up by signs from Washington that the corporations he represents—everything from Chevron to Liberty Bank to Coca-Cola—were about to receive a package of tax breaks, subsidies and relaxed regulations so generous it would make the job of a lobbyist virtually obsolete" (Klein, October 10, 2005). What views did Mr. Drennen offer on the poor, mostly Black residents from the Ninth Ward and other poor sections of New Orleans who had been flooded out and lost everything? Klein further noted, "Listening to Drennen enthuse about the opportunities opened up by the storm (Katrina), I was struck by his reference to African-Americans in New Orleans as 'the minority community.' At 67% of the population, . . . while whites like Drennen make up just 27%. It was no doubt a simple verbal slip, but I couldn't help feeling that it was also a glimpse into the desired demographics of the new and improved city being imagined by its white elite . . . I honestly don't know and I don't think anyone knows how they (the Black poor of New Orleans) are going to fit in,' Drennen said of the city's unemployed." Klein went further in describing Drennen's reflections on the New Orleans poor by noting "As for the hundreds of thousands of residents whose low-lying homes and housing projects were destroyed by the flood, Drennen points out that many of those neighborhoods were dysfunctional to begin with. He says the city now has an opportunity for 'twenty-first-century thinking'; rather than rebuild ghettos, New Orleans should be resettled with 'mixed income' housing, with rich and poor, Black and white living side by side" (Klein, 2005). At the very least there appears to be a close relationship between the mayor and the white power structure of New Orleans. But there is no such interaction between the elites and the mostly Black Ninth Ward and other mostly Black wards within the Big Easy. Clearly the Mayor of New Orleans has chosen to go the route of many Black mayors in larger cities in his constructing a relationship with big business and the corporate elite to rebuild New Orleans.

I believe that the policy of intentional neglect toward the plight of the poor, who in New Orleans case happen to be predominantly Black, is the way business is done at all levels of government. This includes neglecting the maintenance of the levees and canals surrounding New Orleans. The intentional neglect was practiced mostly by Federal officials, who cut the funds needed for the upkeep of these levees and canals. Intentional neglect was displayed by state and local officials toward the Ninth Ward and other sections of New Orleans. The fact that local and state officials were not better prepared to address the need of these communities before Katrina struck not only showed incompetence in specifically dealing with the storm victims, but also is a norm of dismissiveness toward these poor and politically/socially vulnerable communities.

The societal climate supporting the government's intentional neglect of poor people is not new. It contributes to that lack of urgency and competence demonstrated by public officials at all levels of government in New Orleans. This climate of intentional neglect, which cannot be detected by the meteorologists at the National Hurricane Center, challenges the notion that it is *simply* mean-spirited white racist officials who were unwilling to take the time to bring help to these poor Black people of New Orleans. Black people are of course, after many many years of historical experience, rightly suspicious about the intentions of the Bush administration. Black people are generally more politically astute than many of their white counterparts about where the conservative-dominated government really stands when it comes to the public good. But statements such as "George Bush don't like Black people" and "If these victims had been white, these government agents would have responded more aggressively and quickly" do not fully capture the overall long-term strategic conservative attack on a socially beneficial infrastructure that should be in place to help everyday people of all races and ethnicities, but which is now decidedly weakened. Many people of color have no difficulty understanding that they are on the hit list of the expendable and the vulnerable. Others might think that their lighter color will offer them some protection despite their low-income working-class status (and often it does) even though it is their children who die at greater rates than the children of white millionaires in America's wars; and it is their families that face the world without the everyday protections afforded to the rich and the powerful. The basic fact is that if the population had been 67% mostly poor white, with no real say in New Orleans or Louisiana politics, intentional neglect would still drive the official responses, and the disaster would have probably been quite similar to the nightmare that actually took place.

References

Cooper, Christopher. "Old Line Families Escape Worst of Flood and Plot the Future," *Wall Street Journal*, September 8, 2005.

Davis, Mike and Anthony Fontenat. "25 Questions About the Murder of New Orleans," *The Nation* (Web only), posted September 30, 2005.

Duke, Lynne and Teresa Wiltz. "A Nation's Castaways," *Washington Post,* September 4, 2005.

Klein, Naomi. "Purging the Poor," *The Nation*, October 10, 2005.

Robinson, Eugene. *Washington Post* Writers Group, "Bennett baggage may be our own," in the *San Francisco Chronicle,* p. B7, October 4, 2005.

Editor's note: See also Adolph Reed Jr.'s "The Real Divide" in *The Progressive*, November 2005, published after this chapter was written.

30

In Our Blood, In Our Bones

Carolyn Dunn

Many people are expressing outrage over the (non)response of the Federal and local governments to the refugees of Hurricane Katrina immediately preceding the destruction of the Gulf Coast states of Louisiana, Mississippi, and Alabama. Indecision, lack of planning, intimidation, and genocide have a historical presence in this country. If we think that what occurred in New Orleans was not a forced relocation of a population then we are sorely mistaken. If people don't understand the stranding of people of color as an organized method of genocide, then we need to look to our colonial past and present for clues.

Yes, genocide. In the comfort of our living rooms, the rest of the country (and the world) watched in absolute horror as people were left to die in the streets and in the convention center in New Orleans. Two weeks after the hurricane, many of the eight communities of the Mississippi Band of Choctaw Indians were still without power and phone service; and according to Brenda Norrell in her September 9 piece in *Indian Country Today*, three-quarters of the Houma Indian population were directly affected by the hurricane's destruction. Louisiana's other tribes subsist primarily on the fishing industry, which is all but destroyed.

Genocide is nothing new in Indian country; the faces I saw on the news dying in the streets of New Orleans looked amazingly familiar. These are faces I know in my bones. They are the ancestors left to die after a government promised them food, clothing and shelter. They are the ancestors whose rotting bodies were left to the elements, sometimes snow, sometimes rain; this time in heat and hostile waters. I was moved by the account of New Orleans refugee Denise Moore, trapped at the Convention Center with her mother, her niece, and her niece's two-year-old daughter. Denise spoke of being without food and water, without help; babies and elders dying around her. Denise watched National Guard trucks filled with water drive by, weapons pointed at the survivors trapped there. "The story became 'they just left us here to die,'" she told Ira Glass on *This American Life*. How could the refugees have thought anything else? The Federal government has a long and violent colonial history in which native peoples were forcibly removed from ancestral homelands, sent away in the worst possible environmental conditions, left to die without food, water, shelter, or sanitary conditions, and forced to stay in a place that was supposed to be safe.

People who tried to leave the Convention Center in New Orleans were being forced to return by the National Guard. Those refugees there knew that colonial history; they lived it day to day like native peoples live it. The Japanese Americans interred during World War II on the west coast of the United States were forced out of their homes at gunpoint and sent to remote desert areas in California, Nevada, Utah, and Arizona. The Army and the National Guard set up barbed wire and towers to guard these Americans and keep them in camp. People died there. People died on The Trail of Tears. People died at Tippecanoe, where Andrew Jackson's regiment slaughtered thousands of Muskogee women, children and elders, making bridle reins of skin, decorated with the teeth and fingers of my ancestors. Wounded Knee, Sand Creek, Captain Jack's Stronghold, Indian Island, Marana, Topaz, New Orleans . . . our ancestors reminded us of what was to come.

My mother is Creole and Cajun; her family is from Opelousas, Marksville, and Alexandria. I consider Louisiana to be the old country, the nation that haunts me still, two generations later in California. The Creole diaspora has just had its latest migration, thousands of people expelled in a seeming instant. I was in New Orleans two years ago with my aunt, my children, and my dear friend Paula Gunn Allen. We stayed downtown, did touristy things like going to the French Quarter, drinking chicory and eating beignets served by Vietnamese waitresses at Café du Monde, and walking through Jackson Square and posing for pictures with the balloon man. But I took my children to the riverwalk and looked out at the dark water. "This is our grandmother," I told them, "this is where we come from, me and your dad and you guys and your grandparents and great-grandparents and great-great-grandparents and great-great-great-grandparents all the way back to the Mounds and back to Acadia and back to France and back to Africa. This river is our grandmother." My children, at the time seven, two, and ten months, looked at the water, then my son said, "Yeah, OK, Mama, can we get a balloon animal now?" We could have been Denise Moore and her mother, her niece, her great-niece. We could have been that family trapped by skin color and minimum-wage existence in rising flood waters. And like Denise Moore, we survived genocide.

We try so hard to provide a good life for our children, my husband and I do. We learned that from our ancestors in bone and blood, on both sides of the Mississippi River. On both sides is a history saturated with colonial violence, survivance, and renewal. Natural disasters are nothing new to us. This we can cope with. This we know in our blood, in our bones. Unfortunately, we know genocide when we see it.

I know about ethnic cleansing and population control, and it doesn't always happen in faraway places such as Bosnia and Rwanda. Safely in Los Angeles, if that can even be truly said, I watch and listen to the story I know that is going to be told. We have been told that words carry a life of their own; once they are spoken one can never "take them back." As people kept talking and talking about the horror and the devastation, children and babies and grandmas and grandpas and aunties and uncles and mommas and daddies died, waiting for help that never came. This is a familiar story. But the other story, the one that not many people outside of Indian Country know about, is the story of survivance within that death.

The Last Indian in the World

When all is
said and done,
there are no hearts left
in the world
but white heart beads,
fragments of broken glass,
china cups
chipped and worn in places where teeth
stain the delicate
turquoise rims.
We need the cups,
she says,
to remember the land,
to remember the place
where from before you came,
a distant memory
alive in the mines that
shine silver,
or some other precious
metal. Skin color,

perhaps,
named for the place
buried in the heart
of your mother,
where ashes now reside
bones picked clean by the
insistent digging of things
not claimed, but stolen,
and you will walk these streets
knowing your claim
will never be
acquiesced.
You speak
for the nation,
she said,
but how can I speak
when the words
cut from my mouth,
lost on a tongue
for whom language
has been lost?
The last Indian in the world
cannot speak for shit.
When she opens her mouth,
blood comes forth
and nothing
can ever replace
what has been lost,
broken,
mined for shine
that never will
be found.

I am certainly not the last Indian in the world, nor will I be, nor will my children be. The African diaspora grew over the last few weeks since Katrina, and those folks spread across the world won't be the last Black folks in the world either. People of color know how to cope. It's in our blood, in our bones. The stories that live there continue on and are told over and over, so we don't forget where we came from. Nothing can replace what was lost, nothing can be found, but at least we're alive. At least the story doesn't end here.

31

For a Collective Individualism: Katrina's Lessons

John Brown Childs

I see one-third of a nation, ill-housed, ill-clad, and ill-nourished. . . .

We knew that a leaderless system of economy had produced and would again produce economic and social disaster . . . Government leadership was the only method left.

—President Franklin Roosevelt,
on the origins of the New Deal, 1937
(cited in Edsforth, 2000, pp. 121, 148)

Government is not the solution to our problems. Government is the problem.

—President Ronald Reagan,
in his 1980 inaugural address

From New Deal to No Deal: Conservatism's Radical Dismantling of Responsible Government

The overwhelming of the New Orleans levees that led to the disastrous flooding of that city after Hurricane Katrina was tragically real and also emblematic of the effects of more than four decades of systemic conservative strategies aimed at radically reducing the role of national government in the overall public well-being. The levees in New Orleans are part of an extensive nationwide Federal Government–managed system of navigable waterways. The Army Corps of Engineers is charged with its maintenance, from navigation aides to levees. As many writers have noted, both before and since Katrina, funding for levee maintenance was cut in recent years. These reductions in spending contributed directly to the lack of strength in the levees which in turn led to the flooding. But such funding cuts are part of a much larger strategic and long-running conservative policy in which support for socially beneficial projects is cut under the banner of "reducing wasteful big government."

So a fundamental issue, rawly exposed by the ravages of Hurricane Katrina, is that of corrosive consequences from reduced Federal government responsibility for public well-being. Paul Krugman correctly observes that the "mission" of President Bush "is to dismantle or at least shrink the federal social safety net" (October 3, 2005, A25). This dismantling is but the latest chapter in a long-running reduction of that governmental responsibility, as a direct result of the dismembering of the Roosevelt New Deal social reconstruction programs, and their later War on Poverty descendants in the 1960s and 1970s. These governmental strategies were heavily influenced by progressive grassroots activism, from civil rights organizers to labor unions. But they at least demonstrated some degree of leaning toward socially responsible government that was much too much for the conservatives.

In understanding the conservative attack on responsible government, it is useful to remember that during the Depression, conservatives, some Republican and some Democrat, engaged in bitter, usually losing, battles with FDR's New Deal emphasis on a major reconstructive societal role for government. By contrast, most progressives, including other Democrats, Republicans, unions, farmers and civil rights organizations (and the progressive Eleanor Roosevelt) saw important potential in the New Deal and pushed it to become even broader. For example, some important African-American organizers such as the highly effective Mary McLeod Bethune and A. Philip Randolph put pressure on FDR to move toward non-racist inclusionary policies, which he partly did. So the New Deal, like the later War on Poverty, was a combination of top-down policy driven in part by major grassroots activism.

The conservatives mostly lost their battle with FDR, but they continued to counterattack against the New Deal and its legacy. With the coming of Richard Nixon to the Presidency, that counterattack gained an important beachhead. But it would not be until the election of Ronald Reagan that this counterattack began to gain significant institutional momentum. The Reagan era marks the beginning of the large-scale forced march away from socially responsible government. The sociologist Daniel Patrick Moynihan had already provided intellectual cover for this ideological direction during the Nixon administration by labeling it "benign neglect," thereby implying that people would benefit from the absence of "too big a government." The conservatives' increasingly radical demolitionist definition of an ever more limited role for public service government (except in some areas like defense spending) forms the basic strategic environment, in which inadequately funded levee repair results in traumatic flooding out of hundreds of thousands of people, many of them poor and therefore already highly vulnerable to social shock.

This wide-ranging impact affected the vulnerable population across a broad spectrum of communities. In addition to the many Blacks, whites and Creoles who were affected, Native Americans, Latinos, communities of Southeast Asian origin, and immigrant workers were among diverse groups who suffered the consequences. All too often the very young, the elderly and those left in flooding jails encountered dire and devastating circumstances. The Congressional Hispanic Caucus reports that about 200,000 Latino immigrants were in the Gulf region when Katrina hit. Some were being subjected to harassment and threats of deportation rather than hurricane recovery assistance. The CHC stated:

> "Immigrant communities in Louisiana, Alabama, and Mississippi face double devastation due to the shortage of emergency information and the ongoing fear of deportation—even for those with proper documentation that may have been lost or destroyed during the storm," said Rep. Ruben Hinojosa, chair of the CHC Education Task Force. "This treatment is deplorable. . . ."
> —Congressional Hispanic Caucus, October 7, 2005

Curtis Muhammed, of Community Labor United in New Orleans, pointed out in an interview on Amy Goodman's "Democracy Now" that ambulances had bypassed the predominately Black Charity Hospital (where the medical staff pleaded for help for days on radio and television but received none). He also noted that official checkpoints had been set up that prevented people from leaving the city "for fear they were going to loot the dry towns, white towns . . . up the road. And they started locking the shelters at night so people could not sneak away" (C. Muhammed, 2005).

And of course the vulnerability caused by having marginal incomes both cut across and tied together many in these populations. As the Choctaw educator Cedric Sunray, writing in the *Native American Times*, observed about the impact on Native Americans:

The word tragedy can hardly signify the extent of the pain being suffered by many in the wake of Hurricane Katrina. While America comes to grips with the enormity of the despair, people, many of them Black, in the previously unheard of Ninth Ward of New Orleans (one of the country's most impoverished ghettos), already understand the touch, taste, and sound of generations of poverty. A poverty created by a very real caste system, which exist here in the United States of America. And Indians are no exception. Indian country has its own Ninth Ward of . . . individuals and families who have been some of the hardest hit over the course of this past week. . . . As communities of primarily impoverished and identifiable Indian people, we have never had the best of what America has to offer. The prosperity parade doesn't march down the roads of our communities. And neither will assistance. Our lack of federal recognition has placed us at the mercy of federal bureaucrats and the Bureau of Indian Affairs. We are the neglected of the neglected. You see, it is easy to forget about people, when you marginalize them and pretend they no longer exist. Just ask the people in New Orleans's Ninth Ward.

—Cedric Sunray, September 6, 2005, 1[1]

So today we see the corrosive consequences of the overall conservative strategy for cutting socially beneficial programs. Consider the now infamous appointment of Michael Brown as head of the Federal Emergency Management Agency (FEMA). Mr. Brown, who resigned after Katrina under a torrent of criticism, had no previous significant professional experience in emergency management. His prior job had been as head of a horse owners association. Of course, non–civil service directors' positions of major agencies are always Presidential appointments. But as Paul Krugman in the *New York Times* points out, under the Bush administration FEMA became a "dumping ground for cronies and political hacks, leaving the agency incapable of dealing with disasters." Moreover, adds Krugman, "FEMA's degradation isn't unique.

---

[1] Among the Native American communities impacted by Hurricane Katrina are the Chitmacha Nation, the Choctaw Nation, the Houma Nation, the Coushatta Nation, the Poarch Creek Nation, and the Tunica-Biloxi Nation.

It reflects a more general decline in the competence of government agencies whose job is to help people in need" (September 19, 2005, A27).

This "general decline" is part of an underlying political agenda of demolition rather than management, a reality that is captured in a post-hurricane statement made by Michael Brown in his testimony to a Congressional subcommittee. In that testimony Brown said, in effect, that the Federal Government was not really responsible for public well-being in major disasters. Such matters should be left to local government, churches, and other voluntary associations. Brown stated:

> And while my heart goes out to people on fixed incomes, it is primarily a state and local responsibility. And in my opinion, it's the responsibility of faith-based organizations, of churches and charities and others to help those people.
> —Public testimony, US Congress, October 2005

The organizations mentioned by Brown, plus many not mentioned, such as labor unions, grassroots groups, and ad hoc relief committees, all made a tremendous effort to organize the outpouring of support from all over the country. But none of these groups can build entire regional flood control systems, nor do they exercise control over vast areas of concern from health to housing and employment to the environment. Moreover, several weeks after Katrina, many local governments in the Gulf region were nearing financial disaster due to the tremendous impact of the catastrophe on their budgets.

Clearly then, there is more to the problem than simply the "cronyism" appointments of loyal supporters and friends by a President. Importantly, both Michael Brown and his Bush-appointed FEMA predecessor, Joe M. Alburgh (former election campaign director for the President), came to their jobs with a standard conservative loathing of government agencies that provide public service, especially when that service is to people of color and the poor of all races. When he was FEMA director, Alburgh derided his own agency as being just another "entitlement program" so placing it alongside other targets of conservative disdain including welfare and public housing. For most conservatives the term "entitlement program" is a code term for "too much government involvement in society." As Mike Davis notes in *Le Monde Diplomatique*, Alburgh, as FEMA director, "took care to amputate a number of principal programs" (my translation; 2005, 4).

The cases of these Bush FEMA directors are but a few among many examples of the appointment of people who are more than cronies. They are actually ideologically opposed to the public service goals of the very agencies with which they have been entrusted. As Jack Krugman argues:

> . . . Housing for Katrina refugees is one of the most urgent problems now facing the nation. . . . But the Department of Housing and Urban Development, which should be the source of expertise in tackling this problem, has been reduced to a hollow shell, with eight of its principal staff positions left vacant (September 19, 2005, A27).

These appointments reflect an overall pattern of institutional dismantlement. As the *New York Times* also pointed out in a September 27, 2005 editorial:

> The gargantuan task of finding permanent housing for the hundreds of thousands of people displaced by Hurricane Katrina will require a policy shift in Congress which has spent the last several years savaging Federal housing programs (A26).

Similarly, Nicolai Ouroussoff notes that the conservative ideologically induced decay of physical infrastructure in New Orleans is part of a nationwide pattern of neglect. Although, as he says, the courageous operators of the city's pumping stations risked their lives to keep the pumps going, they were up against not just the flood but that neglect:

For decades now, we have been witnessing the slow, ruthless dismantling of the nation's urban infrastructure. The crumbling of the levees in New Orleans are only the most conspicuous evidence of this decline: it's evident everywhere, from Amtrak's aging track system to New York's decaying public school buildings. . . . The inadequacy of that vision has now become glaringly obvious. And the problem cannot simply be repaired with reinforcement bars or dabs of cement. Instead our decision makers will have to face up to what our cities have become and why (October 9, 2005, 2 and 25).

David Sirota, in his highly detailed *In These Times* article "Welcome to New Orleans," analyzes the numerous deliberate White House and Congressional policy decisions to weaken emergency response preparation and undermine the flood defenses of New Orleans and other similar protections. Among these decisions:

> February 27, 2001: President Bush proposes a $641 billion cut to the Army Corps of Engineers, including a proposal to provide only half of what administration officials said was necessary to sustain the Southeast Louisiana Flood Control Project.
>
> June 20, 2001: The *Times-Picayune* reports that "despite warnings that it could slow emergency response to future flood and hurricane victims, House Republicans stripped $389 million in disaster relief money from the budget."
>
> February 4, 2002: President Bush proposes a $390 million cut to the Army Corps of Engineers. The cuts come during the same year the richest 5% (those who make an average of $300,000 or more) are slated to receive $24 billion in tax cuts.
>
> February 26–27, 2002: President Bush's Army Corps of Engineers Chief Mike Parker testifies before House and Senate committees that "there will be a negative impact" if the White House cuts to infrastructure are accepted by Congress.
>
> March 7, 2002: Mike Parker is fired.
>
> June 8, 2004: The *Times-Picayune* reports that "for the first time in 37 years, Federal budget cuts have all but stopped major work on the New Orleans area east bank hurricane levees" (Sirota, October 24, 2005, 16, 17, 18).

Sirota concludes, ". . . New Orleans provides only one example of how tax cuts are routinely put ahead of the most pressing public priorities" (October 24, 2005, 37).

In the same vein, Darryl Pinkney writes:

> It is a scandal that it took so long for there to be air drops of any kind. Maybe Bush can't respond convincingly to the calamity because to do so would require thinking, along New Deal lines, of the kind of government agencies and programs that he is ideologically opposed to.
>
> After years of inadequate investment in the country's infrastructure, this could be the first grave consequence of its misspending. The US telephone systems, bridges, railroads, and highways are in poor shape. The authorities were told twenty-five years ago that the New Orleans levees could not withstand a storm of Katrina's magnitude, but a city that votes Democratic wasn't going to get the necessary allocations to refortify them. In fact Bush heavily cut requests for money to strengthen the levees holding back Lake Pontchartrain (2005, 6).

Disturbingly, one of the few areas of quick and efficient government response was the rapid deployment into New Orleans of the private security company "Blackwater," known for its largely unsupervised mercenary or "contractor" guard work in Iraq. Working for the Department of Homeland Security, and sanctioned by the Louisiana Governor, Blackwater's operatives arrived heavily armed and "dressed in full battle gear" not to rescue people but to control them with official "shoot to kill" orders from the state government (Scahill, 2005).[2]

In Contrast: the New Deal Spirit

In contrast to conservative ideology, the original New Deal compact with the people of the United States made tangible

---

[2] Some rescuers involved directly on the ground, notably the US Coast Guard, performed effective and courageous rescue work. The military effort, once the Louisiana-born Creole General Honoré assumed command, began to work more effectively and with more alertness to peoples' needs.

government-led concessions to millions of people, such as the right of workers to strike. The New Deal represented the triumph of what I would call "the concessionary wing of power elite thought"[3] within the political classes that believed real compromises with tangible benefits to the people were essential in order to address dangerous societal crises of the Great Depression. Despite the hostility of other power-elite circles who castigated what they perceived to be the giving "of an inch to those who will take a mile" as being "communist," this New Deal concessionary approach increasingly emphasized inclusion of the previously marginalized. Consequently, there were some real benefits to wide parts of the population who had been excluded or ejected from societal services, opportunities, and protections. As Bruce Seely observes:

> New Deal public works reached every nook and cranny of the country. The PWA (Public Works Administration) alone sprinkled 35,000 projects across the landscape. . . . Towns that had never seen a Federal dollar profited from the New Deal largesse. Wilton, Alabama, for example, received $39,000 from the WPA (Works Progress Administration) to build its first water supply system . . . driven by the need to put people to work, the Federal government now found itself engaged in fields where it never before had been involved. A listing of PWA projects includes many buildings (7,488 schools, 822 hospitals, and 4,287 other public buildings); 2,582 water systems; 1,850 sewer systems; 375 electric power projects; and 470 flood control projects (1993, 32).

During the New Deal, the Civilian Conservation Corps (CCC) provided jobs to hundreds of thousands young men in conservation related construction projects. The CCC was often locally racially restrictive with racial quotas being in place in the South. Somewhat more broadly, the National Youth Administration (NYA) provided work for young women and men living at home or attending college. The NYA's more inclusionary race and gender breadth were

---

[3] I am following Antonio Gramsci in the *Prison Notebooks* here.

largely the result of the above-mentioned civil rights activist Mary McLeod Bethune, who directed the "Negro Affairs" section of the NYA.

The New Deal was severely constrained by prevailing segregationist practices and overall racial inequality, as many writers, such as University of California professor Michael K. Brown (2002), point out. But the New Deal displayed an important awareness, however limited, of the need to reach a broad range of people. As Robert S. McElvaine observes, the New Deal was built on the mobilization of "Blacks, Jews, Catholics, women, intellectuals and independent Republican progressives" who joined "with labor and the traditional Democratic [Party] strength in the city machines and the south" (1993, 279–280).

At its best the New Deal was premised on the core principles of socially responsible government, and of inclusion rather than exclusion. Secondly, the New Deal was based on the provision of actual tangible benefits such as jobs, training, and education to millions of individuals. Thirdly, these benefits were also directed at contributing to the general public well-being through the building of the social/physical structures of society. So, for example, when young women and men in the Civilian Conservation Corps and the National Youth Administration programs received jobs, skills, and education they did so as they helped to build necessary infrastructure and as they helped to enhance the social and cultural makeup of the society.

A Twenty-First Century Alternative— Collective Individualism and Transcommunal Cooperation

The New Deal, and the later War on Poverty, were of course products of their time. We cannot simply try to recreate them in this the beginning of the twenty-first century. Moreover, knowing what we do about their limitations and weaknesses, we would not want such duplication. But we can reinvigorate the core progressive and inclusionary New Deal spirit for today. The essence of that spirit is the "win-win" proposition that government-provided benefits to individuals can also be benefits to society. And of course, since "society" means all the people, then it is millions of individuals who gain from those benefits. In effect this is a positive circle of constructive pathways from the individual to the societal and from the societal to the individual. We can call this circularity a form of *Collective Individualism.*[4]

It is collective insofar as the benefits (such as jobs and job training) must to a large extent come with the cooperation of government, especially the national government, if they are to reach large numbers of people. And there must be a broad societal or collective will to provide these benefits. It is also collective because the benefits flow back into society. Many benefit from the construction of public hospitals, schools, water systems, and environmental rehabilitation and flood control that are constructed by individuals who in turn are gaining from the jobs and job training. To the degree that individuals and society at large are shielded to some extent from disasters, the cost of post-disaster recovery is actually lessened—meaning that overall tax dollars are better spent with a great return to all who pay them. At the same time the benefits are also aimed at helping the individual to have a decent life of meaningful work. The benefits give those who lack the buffers of great wealth the means to face the inevitable human crises of life while enhancing people's ability to creatively develop.

In its emphasis on the *individual,* "Collective Individualism" avoids the heavy-handed totalitarian forms of failed state communism that crushed individual freedom and initiative. At the same time, in its positive emphasis on the *collective,* this

---

[4]For one example of this outlook, see the proposal for an "Ethical Reconstruction Commission" by Johnson in this book, p. 65.

term also goes against the ruthless privatized dog-eat-dog, everyone-for-themselves mentality of unbridled capitalism.

We can move toward a twenty-first-century form of Collective Individualism which, rather than creating more burdensome bureaucracy, establishes effective relationships between responsible government and the thousands of community groups now active in many urban and rural settings. This Collective Individualism would contain key elements from the past, notably the willingness to effectively bring to bear the tremendous resources to which only the national government has access. But this community-based approach will differ from the "old" New Deal in its emphasis on respectful working partnerships with communities, grassroots groups, and other organizations such as unions. Local knowledge shaped by real experience can provide sharp insights into the real world.

Proactive, public service–oriented national government is vital. National government is important because local communities are, for better or worse, locked into wide-ranging, often globalized, economic/social/technological networks (think about electric power grids, fuel supplies, and global epidemics). No nation, let alone a local community or organization, can deal in isolation with all aspects of such wide-ranging deep-seated systems. So community organizations and local institutions, no matter how effective, need partnerships with national government. But government needs partnerships with communities if its programs are to be effective, accepted, and meaningful.

We are actually now well-positioned to push toward a Collective Individualism format for twenty-first-century US society. We have learned from the nightmarish consequences of totalitarian states both of the left and the right, with their overwhelming emphasis on the totality of society against the freedom of the individual and against cultural diversity. But we also see the worldwide corrosive impacts of government policies supporting without reservation the for-profit economic empires that destroy body and soul, earth, air, and water in the name of huge profits for a few. We are fully aware of the dire consequences of embedded racism and exclusion. We know the need for broad inclusionary approaches. And, after decades of social movement action from many different angles in the United States, we are in a positive political grassroots environment with thousands of effective community organizations in place. Moreover, we are now more than ever before aware of the importance of recognizing human diversity as a basic reality. "Multiculturalism" as an outlook may have its limitations and difficulties. But the *multicultural reality* of this highly heterogeneous world needs to be worked with rather than denied. This recognition opens the way for inclusionary, constructive interactions among many different types of organizations and communities. Many of these groups, such as Community Labor United in New Orleans, working in wide-ranging networks, demonstrate that there are effective ways already in place to maintain particularistic rooted affiliations, while also creating broad constellations of inclusive cooperation that draw from, rather than obliterate, diversity—I call this way of cooperation *transcommunality.* By "transcommunality" I mean the constructive and developmental interaction occurring among distinct and highly autonomous communities and organizations, each with its own history, outlook, and agenda. Transcommunality views these diverse group settings as bases for, rather than obstacles to, cooperation (Childs 1997, 2003). So a Collective Individualism, inspired by the win-win spirit of the New Deal, and based on constructive transcommunal interaction among a wide range of communities and organizations, can be a foundation upon which responsible national government will be willing and able to provide genuine public service.

We, the diverse peoples of the United States, must push for a revitalization of the New Deal spirit as a Collective Individualism for the twenty-first century. As we do so, we can draw our strength from the many organizational advances that have been made over several decades, while also electing responsive and responsible progressives to government from the local to the national levels.

References

Brown, Michael K. *Political Culture and Antipoverty Policies in the New Deal and Great Society.* University of California Santa Cruz, Center for Justice, Tolerance, and Community Working Paper Series, 2002.

Childs, John Brown. *Transcommunality: from the Politics of Conversion to the Ethics of Respect.* Philadelphia, Temple University Press, 2003.

———. "Transcommunality: A Twenty-First-Century Social Compact for Urban Revitalization in the United States," Ed. Jean-Michel Lacroix. *Villes et Politiques Urbaines au Canada et aux États-Unis.* Paris, Sorbonne University Press, 1997.

Congressional Hispanic Caucus, "Hispanic Caucus Demands Administration Honor its Word to Protect All Hurricane Victims" (press release), October 7, 2005. See also the essays by Bravo/García (p. 57) and Aptheker (p. 48) in this book.

Davis, Mike,. "Capitalisme de catastrophe." *Le Monde Diplomatique*, October 2005, pp. 1, 4–5.

Edsforth, Ronald. *The New Deal: America's Response to the Great Depression.* Malden, Massachusetts, Blackwell, 2000.

Krugman, Paul. "Tragedy in Black and White," *New York Times*, September 19, 2005, p. A27.

———. "Miserable by Design," *New York Times*, October 3, 2005, p. A25.

McElvaine, Robert. *The Great Depression: America, 1929–1941.* New York, New York Times Books, 1993.

Muhammed, Curtis. "Interview" on Amy Goodman's Democracy Now, 2005.

Ouroussoff, Nicolai, 2005. "How the City Sank," *New York Times*, October 9, Section 2, pp. 1, 35. See also Bob Herbert's insightful commentary in his regular column in *The New York Times.*

Pinckney, Darryl. "On Our Own," *New York Review of Books*, October 6, 2005, p. 6 (originally published in the *Guardian*).

Scahill, Jeremy, 2005. "Blackwater Down," *The Nation*, October 10, pp. 18–20. Good reporting on this issue also appeared on Amy Goodman's independent news program "Democracy Now." Blackwater's presence was directly related to the exaggerated claims of Black criminality and looting. As Earl Ofari Hutchison pointed out, "Those in the media, and public officials such as Nagin, that ignored evidence to the contrary, and spread wild tales of rape, murder, and mayhem, edged dangerously close to demonizing thousands of Blacks. . . ." ("Race, Lies, and New Orleans," *The Michigan Citizen*, October 16, 2005).

Seely, Bruce. "The Saga of American Infrastructure," *Wilson Quarterly*, Winter 1993, pp. 18–47.

Sirota, David. "Welcome to New Orleans: How the Katrina catastrophe proves that the conservatives' tax cut zealotry has left America vulnerable to disaster," *In These Times*, October 24, 2005, pp. 16–21, 36.

Sunray, Cedric. "Similarities between Tribes and the Ninth Ward," *Native American Times*, September 6, 2005, p. 1. Amy Goodman in her "Democracy Now" program also did excellent interviews and reporting on the Indigenous peoples of the Gulf and Hurricane Katrina. See also the essays by Dunn (p. 153) and Aptheker (p. 48) in this book.

Contributors

David Anthony is Associate Professor of History at the University of California Santa Cruz, where he focuses on African and African-American histories. Among his many writings is the recent book *Max Yergan: Race Man, Internationalist, Cold Warrior* (2006). He is co-editor, along with Robert R. Edgar and Robert T. Vinson, of the forthcoming New York University Press book *Crossing the Water: African-American Historical Linkages with South Africa.*

Bettina Aptheker is Professor of Feminist Studies and History at the University of California Santa Cruz. She is the author of, among many works, *The Morning Breaks: The Trial of Angela Davis* (1976/1999) and *Woman's Legacy: Essays on Race, Sex, and Class in American History* (1982). Her new book *Intimate Politics: Autobiography as Witness* will appear in Spring 2006.

Eduard van de Bilt teaches history in American Studies at the University of Leiden in the Netherlands. He holds a PhD in history from Cornell University. Among his works are *Becoming John Adams: Leiden and the Making of a Great American, 1780–1782* (2005) and *Newcomers in an Old City: The American Pilgrims in Leiden, 1609–1620,* with Johanna Kardux (1998/2001).

Grace Lee Boggs is a Detroit-based activist, writer, and speaker whose more than sixty years of political involvement encompasses the major US social movements of the twentieth century. Her autobiography, *Living for Change* (University of Minnesota Press, 1998), is widely used in university classes on social movements, Detroit history, and Asian-American studies.

José T. Bravo is the Executive Director of the Just Transition Alliance, based in San Diego, California. JTA is a voluntary coalition of labor, economic and environmental justice activists, indigenous people, and working-class people of color, organized around safe workplaces and environments for healthy viable communities within a sustainable economy. (justtransition@sbcglobal.com)

Jeremy Brecher co-edited (with John Brown Childs and Jill Cutler) *Global Visions: Beyond the New World Order* (1993) and *In the Name of Democracy: American War Crimes in Iraq and Beyond* (2005). He has authored numerous works, including *Strike!* (1997) and *Globalization from Below* (with Tim Costello and Brendan Smith; 2000).

Michael K. Brown is Professor of Politics at the University of California Santa Cruz. He is the author of *Race, Money, and the American Welfare State* (1999) and coauthor of *Whitewashing Race: The Myth of the Color-Blind Society* (2003).

Heather Bullock is Associate Professor of Social Psychology at the University of California Santa Cruz, where she works on how social-economic position shapes the understanding of poverty, wealth and economic justice issues. Among many works she is author of "From the frontlines of welfare reform: An analysis of social worker and welfare recipient attitudes" in the *Journal of Social Psychology* (2004), and coauthor of "Media images of the poor" in the *Journal of Social Issues* (2003).

Wendy Cheng is an artist, geographer, and doctoral student in American Studies and Ethnicity at the University of Southern California.

John Brown Childs is Professor of Sociology at the University of California Santa Cruz. He is author of *Leadership, Conflict, and Cooperation in Afro-American Social Thought* (1989), and the recent *Transcommunality: From the Politics of Conversion to the Ethics of Respect* (2003). He serves on the Board of Directors of Communities for a Better Environment in California and served previously on Boards of Directors for the Advocacy Institute and the Preamble Initiative in Washington, DC; Barrios Unidos in Santa Cruz; and the Esperanza Education Project in Watsonville,

California. In 1997 he was awarded the Fulbright Thomas Jefferson Chair of Distinguished Teaching at the University of Utrecht in the Netherlands. (jbchilds@ucsc.edu)

David Cohen is cofounder of the Advocacy Institute and a Senior Fellow at Civic Ventures and Experience Corps. For well over forty years he has worked on major public issues in the United States as an organizer, lobbyist, and CEO. He has also worked collaboratively with social justice advocates in the United States, Africa, Asia, Latin America, the Middle East, and in Eastern and Central Europe. His advocacy writings have been translated into thirteen languages. He is coauthor of *Advocacy for Social Justice: A Global Action and Reflection Guide* (2001).

Michelle Denise Commander was formerly in the English Department of Florida State University. She is currently an Irvine Fellow in the American Studies and Ethnicity Doctoral Program at the University of Southern California. She is the Managing Editor of the *American Quarterly.*

Guillermo Delgado-P., Latin-American scholar and indigenous rights activist, is originally from the Bolivian Andes. He teaches in the Latin American and Latino Studies Department at the University of California Santa Cruz. He is the author of many works, including "Ethnic Politics and the Popular Movements"; *Identidad, ciudadanía y participación popular desde la colonia al siglo XX* (2003); and coauthor of *Quechua Verbal Artistry: The Inscription of Andean Voices / Arte Expresivo Quechua: La Inscripción de Voces Andinas (*2004). He is the General Editor of *The Bolivian Research Review,* the online journal of the Bolivian Studies Association. (www.bolivianstudies.org)

Carolyn Dunn is wife, mother, poet, journalist, musician, and playwright living in Southern California. She is of Cherokee, Muskogee Creek, Seminole, French Creole, and Cajun ancestry. The author and editor of several works about American Indian literature, she is a member of the all-woman drum group The Mankillers, and is an Irvine Fellow at the Center for American Studies and Ethnicity at the University of Southern California.

William Russell Ellis, Jr. is Professor Emeritus of Architecture at the University of California Berkeley. He focuses on the social aspects of architecture and urban design. He served as a Dean in the College of Environmental Design and as Vice Chancellor for Undergraduate Affairs at UC Berkeley. His works include *Architect's People* (edited with Dana Cuff; Oxford University Press, 1989)—a work that deals with architects' and planners' conceptions of the people who occupy their designs and plans; and *Race Change and Urban Society* (edited with Peter Orleans; Sage Publications, 1971).

Hardy T. Frye is a native of Alabama. He is Professor of Sociology (ret.) at the University of California Santa Cruz. He was an organizer in Mississippi and Alabama for the Student Nonviolent Coordinating Committee (SNCC) during the Civil Rights era; Frye is author of *Black Parties and Political Power: a Case Study* (1980), among other works. He served for two years as Country Director of the Peace Corps in Guyana. He was an advisor to Gus Newport, the first African-American mayor of Berkeley.

Arnoldo García works for the National Network for Immigrant and Refugee Rights, based in Oakland, California. The NNIRR is a national organization composed of local coalitions and immigrant, refugee, community, religious, civil rights and labor organizations and activists. It serves as a forum to share information and analysis, education, and plans of action to promote just immigration and refugee policies and the rights of all immigrants and refugees regardless of immigration status. (agarcvia@nnirr.org)

Herman Gray was born and raised in Florida. He is Professor of Sociology at the University of California Santa Cruz, and author of numerous works, including: *Producing Jazz: The Experience of an Independent Record Company* (1988); *Watching Race: Television and the Struggle for Blackness* (1995); and most recently *Cultural Moves: African Americans and the Politics of Representation* (2005).

Rebecca Hall received her PhD in history at the University of California Santa Cruz. Her thesis is entitled *Not Killing Me Softly: African-American Women, Slave Revolts, and Historical Constructions of Racialized Gender* (2004). She also graduated from Boalt Hall School of Law at the University of California Berkeley, after which she represented low-income families for seven years in the areas of housing law and anti-discrimination cases. She now works on the historical formations of racialized gender, legal history, and the legacies of slavery. She is currently a Mellon Post-Doctoral Fellow at UC Berkeley's Center for Race and Gender.

Sharon Howell is a community activist in Detroit, where she has lived for more than thirty years. She works with a number of community-based women's and LGBT organizations and is cofounder of Detroit Summer, a youth leadership organization. She writes a weekly column for the *Michigan Citizen* and is a frequent speaker on community issues. She is Professor of Communication at Oakland University and Chair of the Department of Rhetoric, Communication, and Journalism.

Andrew Jolivette is Assistant Professor of American Indian Studies at San Francisco State University. A native of Louisiana, he is finishing a book on the significance of the Creole population for our understanding of race, culture, and identity in the United States.

Rev. Nelson Johnson is the Executive Director of the Beloved Community Center of Greensboro, North Carolina. The BCC works with the poor and disenfranchised in Greensboro, and takes on a wide range of issues from inadequate housing to education, all focused on community justice. He is also a member of the Interfaith Worker Justice network of people of all faiths working on behalf of improving conditions for workers, especially low-income workers. Rev. Johnson and his wife Joyce Johnson were honored with the Ford Foundation's Leadership for a Changing World award in 2005 for their work in the BCC.

Johanna Kardux is a Professor of English literature in American Studies in the Netherlands at the University of Leiden. She writes on nineteenth-century African-American literature and culture, and on slavery monuments and public memory. Among her many works are "Witnessing the Middle Passage: Trauma and Memory in the Narratives of Olaudah Equiano and Venture Smith and in Toni Morrison's *Beloved*" (in Maria Diedrich, et al., *Mapping African America: History, Narrative Formation, and the Production of Knowledge)* and *Newcomers in an Old City: The American Pilgrims in Leiden, 1690–1620,* with Eduard van de Bilt (1998/2001).

Norma Klahn is Professor of Literature at the University of California Santa Cruz with a focus that includes Mexican literature, Latin American literature, and culture and feminist theories. She is author, editor, and co-editor of numerous works, including: *Los Novelistas Como Criticos* (1991); *Las Nuevas Fronteras del Siglo XXI* (2000); and *Chicana Feminisms: A Critical Reader* (2003). She is an organizing founder and former co-director of the Chicano/Latino Research Center at the University of California Santa Cruz.

Rabbi Michael Lerner is the editor of *Tikkun*. He is the author of, among many works, *Jewish Renewal: A Path to Healing and Transformation* (1994), as well as the forthcoming book on progressive spiritual politics, *The Left Hand of God* (2006).

Rachel E. Luft is a sociologist at the University of New Orleans. She studies race, gender, and social movements, and works with community-based organizations. She evacuated from Katrina, and what she was able to retrieve from her flooded apartment fits in a milk crate.

Wynton Marsalis, composer, musician, and educator, is Artistic Director of Jazz at Lincoln Center. He was born and raised in New Orleans. He is serving on the mayor's Bring Back New Orleans Commission for the rebuilding of New Orleans. In 1997 Marsalis became the first jazz musician to receive a Pulitzer Prize, for his oratorio *Blood on the Fields.* In 2005 he was awarded the National Medal of Arts.

Manulani Aluli Meyer is the fifth daughter of Emma Aluli and Harry Meyer. She hails from a large family dedicated to raising the Hawaiian Nation. She works in the field of philosophy, teacher education, and charter school development. Her book *Ho'oulu: Our Time of Becoming* (2003) summarizes thoughts on Hawaiian epistemology and indigenous ideas of research and hermeneutics. She earned her doctorate from Harvard on the topic of Hawaiian epistemology.

Stan Oden is Assistant Professor in the Department of Government at California State University, Sacramento. He is member of the Board of Directors of the Freedom Bound Center in Sacramento and a founding member of the John George Democratic Club in Oakland, California.

Paul Ortiz is Associate Professor in the Community Studies Department at the University of California Santa Cruz. He is coauthor of *Remembering Jim Crow: African Americans Tell About Life in the Segregated South* (2003). His newest book is *Emancipation Betrayed: The Hidden History of Black Organizing and White Violence in Florida from Reconstruction to the Bloody Election of 1920* (2005). He has worked as a volunteer organizer with the United Farm Workers in Washington State and the Farm Labor Organizing Committee in North Carolina. He is currently writing a book on the history of race and class oppression in the United States.

Curtis Reliford was born and raised in the African-American community of Shreveport, Louisiana. He now lives in Santa Cruz, California. He is a businessman-landscaper, and head of Country Gentleman's Landscaping in Aptos, California. He organized major collections of relief supplies for the survivors of the hurricane and then drove these supplies two times to Louisiana by truck convoy from California. He is an active member of the NAACP and Brothers Helping Brothers in Santa Cruz.

Rickie Sanders is Professor of Geography and Urban Studies and a Fellow in the Society of Fellows in the Humanities at Temple University. She also served as Director of Women's Studies at

Temple. Among her many writings are *Growing Up in America: An Atlas of Youth in America* (with Mark Mattson; 1998); "African Cities in Crisis: Managing Rapid Urban Growth" in *The Geography of Urban Rural Interaction in Developing Countries* (1990); and "Integrating Race and Ethnicity into Geographic Gender Studies," in *The Professional Geographer* (1991).

Andrea Steiner is a faculty member in the Community Studies Department at the University of California Santa Cruz. A gerontologist and health policy analyst, she serves on the board of directors of the Seniors Council of Santa Cruz and San Benito County, and works with the Santa Cruz chapter of the American Civil Liberties Union.

David Wellman is Professor of Community Studies at the University of California Santa Cruz. He is the author of *Portraits of White Racism* (1977); *The Union Makes Us Strong: Radical Unionism on the San Francisco Waterfront* (1997); and is coauthor of *Whitewashing Race: The Myth of the Color-Blind Society* (2003).

William Sakamoto White is Professor of Sociology at the University of New Orleans and is a DJ at radio station WWOZ. He and his family are now "settled into a small, rural, nearly all-white town in Tennessee near Knoxville," where he wrote his essay for this book.